WE'R
BUSI

English for commercial practice and international trade

Teacher's Book

Susan Norman

Longman

Longman House, Burnt Mill, Harlow,
Essex CM20 2JE, England
and Associated Companies throughout the world.

First published 1983
Twelfth impression 1995

ISBN 0-582-74873-9

Set in Linotron 202 9/10 Plantin and Helvetica
Produced through Longman Malaysia, TCP

COURSE CONTENT

We're In Business components:
Students' Book (SB)
Teacher's Book (TB)
Workbook (WB)
Cassette of listening exercises
Two cassettes of laboratory drills (LD)

Other abbreviations used in the TB to save space are:
LDT – laboratory drills tapescript (in TB)
T teacher
S student
SS students
T–S teacher–student (see note on pairwork on TB pages xvii–xix)

We're In Business is a course in English for commercial practice and international trade at early intermediate level.

The course is aimed at SS embarking on the study of English for a business career. It can be used either as a sequel to *We Mean Business* or independently of it. The starting level is post-elementary/early intermediate. However, SS with a greater knowledge of English will also find this book useful as an introduction to the business and commercial information it contains.

The course is designed to provide between 60 and 90 contact hours plus homework, although the amount of time it takes to cover the material will vary from class to class and will depend on whether the additional exercises and optional material are used.

Language content

The grading of the language content is structural, each structure being contextualised in a specific situation and expressing a specific language function. The practice of question forms (which are often neglected in T–S interaction) is greatly increased by the emphasis throughout the course on pairwork. SS are also expected to give short natural answers to questions, rather than 'full sentences' for the sake of extra structure practice which would be highly unnatural. The structural approach is simplified by the introduction of only one main concept at a time for any structure and the emphasis throughout is on the acquisition of relevant and useful language practised in a meaningful context.

Much of the classwork is designed to improve SS' communicative ability, fluency and oral mastery of the language. However, throughout the course, there are also exercises which highlight the skills of reading, writing, listening and pronunciation. The aim within each unit has been to provide a variety of interesting exercises which lend themselves to stimulating classroom exploitation, but which are flexible enough to be used in a variety of teaching systems. Suggestions for presentation and exploitation of the material, suitable h/w activities and further activities are given in the TB. The contents list sets out the language content of the course in detail and the aim of each exercise is stated in the TB.

Business and commercial content

Business English is the language used by people involved in business. Commerce is the study of the procedures which are followed in trade and related activities. This book combines a course in commercial procedures (and an introduction to the related vocabulary) with practice of the written and spoken language typical of business people. **Throughout the course there is an emphasis on helping SS understand *why* the commercial procedures are as they are (they have all evolved from the needs of people engaged in trade). This will help SS (a) remember the information and (b) reconstruct any information they might forget.** The commercial and business language is simplified; introduced gradually and then recycled and revised throughout the course.

Particular attention is paid to the introduction, and understanding, of a wide range of documentation (which SS are otherwise unlikely to see) and to the accompanying correspondence. A substantial number of forms are in the WB, to give SS the opportunity to practise filling them in.

Many TT of commercial English have a literary or academic, rather than a commercial background. If you are unsure of the business or commercial content, work through the exercises in the SB as if you are a S (a) to familiarise yourself with the information and (b) to give you an idea of how difficult or easy the exercise might be for the SS. Then read the additional background information in the TB. Remember that the commercial information in this book is deliberately simplified. Once SS are familiar with the basic information and vocabulary in this book they will find it easier to cope with the complexities of each subject area they need to study in depth later.

Note that the commercial content of this book is accurate according to British law at the time of going to press. However laws change, practice changes with time and procedures vary from country to country and even between companies.

For further practice in office skills and numbers see *Office Practice* (Longman *World at Work* Series) by the same author and *Count Me In* by Steve Elsworth (Longman). For more specialised subjects see *Import Export* by Vicki Hollett and *Banking* by Lynne Rushton and Tony Hopwood (both in the Longman *World at Work* Series). These books are all at early intermediate level and their design and methodological approach is consistent with that in this course.

We're In Business: Students' Book

The SB contains 15 main units, three consolidation units and the listening cassette tapescript. The contents list reproduced in both SB and TB details the language and business content of each unit.

Main units: The first exercise in each main unit introduces the main topic and language area exploited more fully in the rest of the unit. The linguistic and commercial information is then built up gradually while practising a variety of language skills and giving SS experience of some of the sorts of tasks which they are likely to be asked to perform if they work in a business environment.

The main language points are summarised in the language notes at the end of each unit. SS can be directed to the language notes to learn selected items before they are presented or practised in class or they can be studied after the classwork (where the emphasis is on communicative oral work) to help SS grasp the grammatical 'rules' and patterns in the language. These notes only reflect language presented in each unit and frequently simplify the grammatical content to make it more accessible to SS, so they cannot be considered comprehensive or an alternative to a grammar book.

Consolidation units: These three units are based on 'news items' taken from the 'radio' (on cassette) and 'newspaper cuttings'. They revise and consolidate structures and lexis presented in previous units in the context of world and local news. No new structures are presented in these units, but SS are exposed to a wider business context and a greater range of vocabulary. They also include a number of 'articles' in the form of cartoons or puzzles. SS can be left to enjoy these alone (the answers are given in the TB for interested SS) or they can be exploited in class. The focus in these units is on the receptive listening and reading skills.

Newspapers and radio news programmes are a rich source of business language frequently available to foreign learners in their own countries, yet both are difficult to understand without help. The consolidation units provide a graded introduction to the news media and many of these exercises could be adapted to exploit real programmes and articles.

Cassette tapescript: SS should be discouraged from reading the tapescript until after they have done the relevant listening exercises. Scripts are printed in full only if they are not included in the body of the SB (the introductory exercises for each unit, for example, are not printed again in the tapescript). Certain of them are printed only in the TB to stop SS taking answers directly from the tapescript.

There is also a word list containing the commercial vocabulary introduced in the book and a list of the irregular verbs used in the course.

We're In Business: Recordings

Listening cassette (): The listening cassette is an integral part of the course, as throughout there is a systematic approach to improving the listening skill. To improve SS' ability to cope with the spoken English they are likely to encounter in real life, some of the characters speak with a slight regional or American accent, but none of these is strong enough to interfere with understanding. On the cassette are recorded the introductory exercise in each unit plus all other listening exercises marked in the SB and TB with the symbol .

Laboratory drills cassette: The LDs are designed to be used in a laboratory where SS can record their responses on tape, but they can also be used in a listening laboratory or in the classroom. The drills are three-phase: prompt, space for SS' response, correct response. The pace of the drills varies, but all the sentences are spoken at a natural speed for native speakers. This may seem fast to foreign learners at first, but they are more likely to achieve natural intonation patterns if they try to imitate the models exactly. All the drills are spoken in a standard southern educated English accent, although different male and female voices are used for variety.

Drills have the same number as the exercise they refer to. Not all exercises are exploited with a drill and some exercises have more than one drill (numbered A, B, C etc). There are no drills relating to the consolidation unit exercises. The LDT is in the TB and the recorded examples for each drill are printed in the SB immediately after the related exercise. Some of the drills are comprehension exercises relating to the SB and SS are sometimes referred to prompts in the exercises, so they should always take their textbooks into the laboratory with them. However, since the drills are to improve oral/aural competence, whenever possible SS should do the drills with their books closed.

Although the drills are an optional part of the course, they are recommended for use with SS or classes who benefit from individual reinforcement of language. The drills allow SS to concentrate on oral precision, especially where the emphasis in classwork is on communication. Not all classes will need to do every drill and the T is recommended to choose those drills most relevant to his/her own SS. Different SS could well do different drills according to their particular needs and problems (the aim of each drill is stated in the LDT).

Drills can be done before or after classroom practice, but the structures and vocabulary they contain should be presented before they are attempted. TT should refer to the LDT in the TB before SS do the drills as they do not always follow the same format as the classroom exercises and may need particular preparation. TT might also use the LD cassettes in class as a model for intonation patterns, the pronunciation of names etc.

To save space, examples (which are repeated on the cassettes) are not written out again in the LDT.

We're In Business: Workbook

Although the WB is an optional course component in that its main function is to consolidate and give further practice in the language and business content presented in the SB, it is strongly recommended that SS use it since it also contains several forms and documents which could not be reproduced in the SB for reasons of space.

The WB also contains three tests to correspond to the consolidation units in the SB. These cover structural items in previous units and may be used either to check attainment after the course of study or to diagnose areas of weakness.

After each test is a list of the commercial vocabulary introduced in the previous five units in case SS want to write their own explanatory notes.

We're In Business: Teacher's Book

The TB contains: Course contents list
Introduction: Course content
Notes on methodology and contents
18 units to correspond to the 18 units in the SB and WB, each containing:
- Contents list for the unit
- Answers and teaching notes
- Suggested additional activities
- LDT and notes on LD (except for consolidation units)
- WB answers

For ease of reference, answers are written immediately after each exercise heading. Where the exercise follows the same format as the LD, the T is referred to the LDT for answers, but sample answers to freer writing exercises such as letters and reports are intended as a guide only. The aim of each exercise is stated before any teaching suggestions and where exercises may not in themselves be sufficient presentation of new language, a method of presentation is suggested. Although the teaching suggestions reflect how the course was intended to be used, TT should exploit the material in any way appropriate to their SS.

Language explanations are given as a guide to the level of explanation necessary for SS. They are simplified and necessarily incomplete, so TT are recommended to use a grammar book such as *A Communicative Grammar of English* by Geoff Leech and Jan Svartvik (Longman) for further reference.

Although the medium of instruction is intended to be English, there are places in the course where certain vocabulary items are most simply explained by translation. With multi-national classes, SS should be allowed to use native-language-English dictionaries at this point. As much as possible, though, SS should be referred to a simplified English-English dictionary such as the *Longman Dictionary of Contemporary English*. The T is recommended to spend some time familiarising the SS (perhaps with the help of the accompanying booklet) with this invaluable source of self-help. The *Longman Dictionary of Business English* may also prove useful to SS and T.

INTRODUCTION TO METHODOLOGY

The following notes explain some of the ideas underlying the material in this course and give suggestions for exploiting the material to best advantage.

- The medium of instruction in the SB is English and the course was designed to be taught in English.
- The course aims to give SS as much opportunity to speak as possible so there are numerous exercises which require pairwork and groupwork. The T should also get into the habit of *eliciting* information from the SS by asking judicious questions rather than telling them everything. Eliciting also has the advantage of checking whether the SS have understood as you go along.
- SS are expected to take responsibility for their own learning, to be self-reliant and to *think* about what they are learning. The T can encourage this attitude by giving them *time* to think before demanding answers and asking questions rather than telling them information.
- If SS are speaking more, they are likely to make numerous mistakes. If the T is not to discourage them from speaking, correction should be kept to a minimum when the aim of the exercise is fluency and the expression of ideas, but can be quite strict when a new language item is being practised.
- When any new item is being taught (be it language or commerce) the book aims to *elicit* from the SS what they know already, get them to *extend* this knowledge by thinking more closely about it and then adding something new. This can be achieved by asking questions about the SS' own experience, then asking 'loaded' questions which lead SS logically to the right answer and finally to giving further information.

Suggestions for specific types of question are given in the TB in the detailed notes after the relevant exercises.

One technique for encouraging SS to think about a subject and to pool the collective knowledge of the class (often surprisingly comprehensive) is *brainstorming*. This involves asking SS to work in small groups and come up with as many ideas as they can in a short time (three to five minutes) on a given subject (eg *cheques* in Exercise 2.8). Each group then quickly explains its ideas to the rest of the class. The conversation can be in the SS native language and the emphasis is on the pooling of the ideas rather than the accuracy of the language.

Working on the assumption that SS should be able to understand more than they can write or say (they can to some extent control and simplify the language they produce, but they have no control over the complexity of written and oral material they are likely to come across), most of the listening material and some of the reading texts in the course are graded at a higher level than the language SS are expected to produce. To counterbalance this and to make the language more accessible, the exploitation exercises are deliberately simple.

Most of the exercises are designed to encourage SS to skim for general meaning or to scan/listen for specific information. In both cases, SS should not worry about words and expressions they do not understand as long as this does not interfere with the task they have to do. Essential vocabulary that SS need to know (and which may have to be pre-taught) in order to carry out the task is stated in the relevant TB notes. TT should not translate the text.

The aim of the course is not that SS should acquire the accent of a native speaker, but that they should be readily understood by other speakers of English. There is not time in a course of this nature to cover in detail all aspects of pronunciation, but this book does try to awaken an awareness of those aspects of pronunciation which prove the greatest barrier to communication. The aim has been to integrate the teaching of pronunciation with other aspects of language and it will help SS if each new structure is presented with a definite stress and intonation (the LD cassettes can be used to provide a model). The emphasis should be first that SS can hear and identify aspects of pronunciation and then that they try to imitate them. The model provided on the LD cassettes is an educated southern English accent. Phonetic script is not used much in the course, but TT might wish SS to understand the phonetic script used in their dictionaries. In this case, the T can introduce the script gradually as work is done on individual sounds.

Puzzles

There are a number of word puzzles in the book which some TT may feel to be unnecessarily frivolous. In fact, although they are meant to be fun and to enliven what can be quite a dull subject, they do have a serious methodological value. They all encourage SS to concentrate on the form and meaning of specific vocabulary and many of them require SS to look back at a reading text or document and think carefully about the meaning of words in context.

Pairwork

Many of the exercises in this course are marked to be done in pairs. Some of the reasons for this are:

- When practising structures, a stimulus and response more closely resembles a conversation than the series of unconnected utterances in most drills. SS are helped to retain the meaning of a structure when it is in context (even a minimal context). This feeling is enhanced by giving SS a choice of response wherever possible.

- Two SS working together are more likely to arrive at correct utterances or solutions than individual SS working alone (as the English saying goes: Two heads are better than one).
- SS can frequently learn as well from one another as from the teacher.
- If SS work together you remove the testing element (with possible failure in front of classmates) that always exists when SS are asked to work alone. This usually has a good effect on SS' confidence and thereby on their linguistic performance. (SS are still required to work individually and produce correct written work for h/w.)
- The whole class gets the chance to practise new structures several times in a short space of time rather than the common T–S situation where a maximum of six SS say sentences while the rest of the class loses interest.
- The focus of the lesson is moved away from the T, which is good for the sake of variety, but also because it puts the responsibility for learning more obviously where it belongs – on the SS.
- The T is free to move around the class helping SS with learning difficulties.

In order to achieve this happy state, there are several simple rules to follow. Everyone must know the form and meaning of the structure they are practising, so this must have been presented beforehand (suggestions are given in the TB) or must be evident from the exercise itself. SS must also be clear about the exact form of the exercise and what they are expected to do, so the stages of setting up pairwork must make this evident:

- Indicate the exercise in the book.
- Give the first stimulus and elicit the correct response from a S (T–S). Give the second stimulus and elicit the response from another S.
- Indicate two other SS (who are not sitting next to one another) to give the next stimulus and response (S–S, also called 'open pairs'). Indicate two other SS sitting apart to do further stimuli-responses.

Up to this stage it is important that everyone hears and pays attention to what is said and that the T corrects SS who make mistakes with the form of the drill or with the structure.

- Indicate that SS work in pairs with the person sitting next to them (SS–SS, or 'closed pairs'). Make sure that SS know to take turns so that both get a chance to say the stimuli and both to say the responses.

It is not necessary to work through the whole exercise before SS work in closed pairs. Once a couple of examples have been done, SS should be able to work out further examples for themselves. Occasionally move SS round so that they work with different partners (a) for variety and (b) so that stronger and weaker SS can help or learn from one another.

Controlled dialogues

Short dialogues are introduced as language which SS might find useful. It is therefore important that they know them by heart and do not simply read them from the book (which also encourages poor intonation). Some dialogues are presented as such, some drills are really in the form of short dialogues and some of the sections from the introductory picture dialogues (or from the tape) are also suitable to teach to SS. With any dialogue, make sure SS are familiar with the main four or five lines by following this procedure (the example is taken from the introductory dialogue to Unit 5):

- Make noise of ringing phone and mime picking up receiver. Elicit suggestions from SS as to what you answer, eg *Mrs X here/76543* (your telephone number) etc. Pick up one acceptable form and ask individual SS to repeat the line.
- Indicate one of the SS to say the line to you and reply with: *Oh hello. Can I speak to Liz please?* (T–S). Repeat this with another S. Drill this second line with all the SS at once. Then you say the first line to a S who should reply with line two.
- Indicate two SS who should say the lines to one another (S–S). Practise these two lines with as many SS as you feel necessary.
- Bring the attention back to yourself and say line one to a S who replies with line two. You then introduce line three in its rightful position: *I'm afraid she's not here at the moment. Can I take a message?* Drill this line on its own, then practise the three lines T–S–T and then S1–S2–S1.
- Bring the attention back to yourself. Indicate a S to say line one to you. Reply with line two so the S says line three, then introduce line four (*No. I'll ring her back later.*) and practise as above.

Once the SS know the four lines you can introduce substitutions, alterations or additions.
For longer dialogues you can allow SS to make notes of the most important words in each line as a memory-jogger.

An alternative presentation is to give one half (alternate lines) of the dialogue to half the class to learn and prepare and the other half to the rest of the SS (you will need to work with both groups at this initial learning stage). SS then mingle (as in a whole class activity – see page xx) and say the dialogue with SS from the other group until they have heard it often enough to have learnt the other half. You can move around the class and help out with obvious difficulties. SS can then try saying the half of the dialogue they did not learn originally until all the SS can take either part.

Groupwork, whole class activities, roleplay, simulations

With all these activities, as with pairwork or groupwork of any kind, the important thing is that SS know (a) what it is they are supposed to be doing, how they can do it and what the aim of the activity is, ie the rules of the activity (b) the language they need to do it. Note that all the SS are working at the same time and that the T is free to move round the groups giving help or noting language errors which may need work later.

When SS are working in small groups (eg Exercise 9.10), the ideal number of people in each group is probably between four and seven. The T should also decide which SS to put together – sometimes random groups, sometimes brighter SS with slower SS so that they can help or learn from one another, sometimes same ability groups together so brighter SS can go further ahead while slower SS are forced to rely on themselves more etc.

To arrange random groups, decide how many groups you want (eg 5 groups of 6 SS). Ask SS to number off round the class from 1 to 5, 1 to 5 etc until everyone has a number between one and five. Then tell all the number ones to get together as a group, all the number twos to be another group, etc. (If you later want these groups to form new groups, eg 10 groups of three SS, ask them to number off again from 1 to 10, 1 to 10 etc group by group. SS then move to their new groups with people of the same number.)

In a *whole class activity*, all the SS move around the classroom to come into contact with as many other SS as possible with whom to practise specific language in a short time (a maximum time for this kind of activity is ten minutes). This is a *practice* activity so it is essential that the language has been pre-taught.

A big advantage of this kind of activity is that SS seem content to repeat phrases again and again in order to complete the task where they would be bored by saying the same phrases three or four times in a more conventional drill. Whole class activities can also have a revitalising effect on a class which has been sitting still for a long period of time.

The two problems which TT frequently mention in connection with pairwork, groupwork and whole class activities are noise and discipline. All language TT can differentiate between 'productive sound' and 'unproductive noise' and so step in to help SS who do not appear to be working on the task in hand. Given that it is generally accepted that SS need a great deal of practice if they are to learn a language effectively, the problem is mainly one of convincing colleagues that these activities are the most effective and efficient ways of giving large numbers of SS maximum practice in minimum time. Colleagues rarely question the efficacy of chorus-drilling, which, while it is not a technique to be ignored, is not as effective as these other three. Similarly, there will always be some discipline problems whatever teaching techniques you employ. In order to minimise the disruptive effect on the rest of the class, SS who will not join in with these activities can be given extra written work to do alone while the other SS carry on with their tasks. The SS being disciplined still have the chance to practise language (in a different way) and perhaps they will decide that the other activities look more fun and so opt to join in productively on subsequent occasions.

Roleplay involves SS in acting out situations from outside the classroom in order to practise the language they will need when they are in that situation. It does not involve any great acting ability, nor does it imply that SS have to 'learn lines'. SS will have to roleplay in a *simulation* which is the contrived situation, a sort of game. The rules for all the simulations in this book are given clearly in the SB and any particular information is given in the TB. Apart from this follow the basic rules for setting up any kind of activity where SS are left to themselves. Although all the SS are working at once, it is possible to stop all the groups except one so that everyone concentrates on the work of these few SS for a short while. See also the note after Exercise 9.10 on TB page 75 about individual SS swapping roles in the middle of a conversation.

Oral (and written) presentation

In business (and in commercial English examinations) people are frequently expected to be able to present information clearly. However when people present information orally they can react to some extent to the reaction of their listeners so if people seem not to have understood the speaker might explain again in different words or give examples to make the point clear. Because a reader can go back and read a written text as often as necessary to get the information, a written text is generally shorter and written without repetition. SS are given a number of chances to practise giving oral presentations (with written back up) throughout the course and it is not necessary for every S to give a presentation every time. However the more presentations each S does, the better they will become at them. All the SS should do the suggested written back up.

Do not tell the SS in advance who will be giving the presentations so that they all prepare them. Do also tell the SS to note the instruction in the SB not simply to read a prepared passage. They can make notes to remind themselves of the main points they want to make, but they should be prepared to put the ideas into English while they are talking.

There is enough information in the SB for SS to be able to give a short presentation on the given subjects, but you could also encourage SS to research additional information or use diagrams on the board to make their talk more interesting.

Extra teacher preparation

Exercises which may need preparatory work or setting up by the T before the lesson are listed below:

Exercise 2.9	A simulation: Buying and selling
Exercise 3.12	Oral (and written) presentation
Exercise 4.7	Correspondence
Exercise 4.11	A simulation: Broking and underwriting
Exercise 6.11	Oral (and (written) presentation
Exercise 7.12	Oral presentation
Exercise 8.10	Oral (and written) presentation
Exercise 9.9	In-tray exercise
Exercise 9.10	Roleplay
Exercise 10.12	A simulation: Speculating
Exercise 12.13	A simulation: Trade negotiations

UNIT ONE

INTRODUCING TRANSWORLD

1

Language:	The alphabet (pronunciation) Present simple tense Present progressive tense Past simple tense *Will* Greetings and introductions Requests
Business/Commerce:	Job advertisements Telephone enquiries Business letter format and terminology The work of a freight forwarder

TEACHING NOTES

Exercise 1.1 Listening comprehension (LD)

Answers: *1–f,h 2–a,d,k 3–l,p 4–g 5–b,e,j,m 6–c,i,n 7–o*

Aim: Listening comprehension; linking of the pronunciation and written form of English names.

Before you do this exercise, look at the introductory picture sequence. Set the scene with the SS by discussing where the dialogue is taking place and who the characters are. Look through the list of English names in Exercise 1.1 and let the SS guess at how they are pronounced. Listen once through to the tape to confirm or correct their pronunciation. Check the vocabulary students might not know by asking questions such as: *If you sell goods to a foreign country, what are the goods called?* (Exports) *Where do you go to catch a plane?* (To the airport) *Where do you go to get on a ship?* (To a port, to the docks) *When you send goods by any form of transport what are they called?* (Freight or cargo) *When you send goods by sea what are they called?* (Seafreight) *When you send goods by air what are they called?* (Airfreight) *When you travel to another country and you take in too many cigarettes, who do you tell?* (A customs official).

Now ask SS to read quickly through Exercise 1.1. Play the tape through once and then ask the SS to work in pairs and try to remember which of the people on the left did which of the things on the right. If necessary play the tape through again for them to check their answers. It is not important that they understand every word on the tape, only that they can do the exercise. Check their answers by asking individuals to give you full sentences. Each sentence must tell you what one of the people did, like this:

T: *a*
S: *Sandra Parr did the photocopying.*

It is important that you check the answers before SS do the next exercise.

The LD for this exercise practises the past tense of verbs in the exercise.

Exercise 1.2 Present simple and present progressive (LD A, B & C)

Answers: *See LDT*

Aim: To differentiate between the two present tenses.

Elicit from the SS when to use each of the present tenses. One of the main uses of the present progressive (also called the present continuous) is to tell about things which are happening now; it is also used to describe what is happening in a picture. (It can also have future reference, but that is outside the scope of this lesson.) The present simple describes what people do every day, regularly or in their jobs.

Practise the two question forms and the word *else* (meaning 'something more') like this:
T: *Anne – everyday*
S1: *What does Anne do?*
T: *Something more?*
S2: *What else does Anne do?*
T: *Nick – now*
S3: *What's Nick doing? e'*
Remember to use the co. acted form *what's* for *what is* in speech. Before the SS do the exercise in closed pairs, prepare them by doing a few of the examples T–S and then in open pairs (see TB introduction pages xvii–xix).

Be firm in your correction of the final 's' of the third person singular in the present simple tense.

Exercise 1.3 Job advertisements

Answers: *1 Anne Bell is a secretary. 2 Sandra Parr is a person Friday. 3 David Thompson is a junior accounts clerk. 4 Liz Shepherd is a senior accounts clerk. 5 Nick Dawson is a customs clerk. 6 Kevin Hughes is an export manager. 7 Jane Long is an airfreight clerk.*

Aim: Reading comprehension.

Make sure the SS know what to do in this exercise, but do not pre-teach any of the vocabulary. The aim is for them to understand the advertisements without necessarily understanding every word. The only problem students might have is the difference between a *senior accounts clerk* (who is in charge of a department and will therefore probably be the person who was in the job before, ie Liz Shepherd) and a *junior accounts clerk*.

As well as collecting the SS' written work, check their answers orally by asking them to give full sentences such as *Anne Bell is a secretary*. Make sure that they use the indefinite article when talking about jobs. Note that within the context of a company, when only one person holds a named job, we use the definite article, eg Graham Davis is *the* assistant manager of Transworld.

Discuss which words helped them work out which person did which job, but do not translate the advertisements word for word.

NB A *person Friday*, or in this case a *girl Friday*, is a person who does all the minor jobs in an office, eg dealing with the post, filing, making tea for visitors, etc. The name comes from Man Friday in Daniel Defoe's *Robinson Crusoe*. Note also that it is illegal in Britain to advertise specifically for a person of either sex, so you frequently see the word 'person' in job advertisements.

rcise 1.4 Synonyms

Answers: *1–d* *2–a* *3–f* *4–c* *5–b* *6–e*

Aim: Comprehension of vocabulary from context.

SS should be able to do this exercise without any help. Note that *call someone* means to telephone them, but *call on someone* means to visit them.

'cise 1.5 Transworld

Answers: The missing words are *imports, transportation, customs, airfreight, seafreight, documentation, exports*.

The numbers in the puzzle stand for the following letters:

1 = E	*2 = O*	*3 = N*	*4 = A*	*5 = F*	*6 = S*
7 = I	*8 = T*	*9 = X*	*10 = C*	*11 = M*	*12 = R*
13 = D	*14 = G*	*15 = U*	*16 = P*	*17 = H*	

Information about Transworld (apart from that already mentioned in the answers to the previous exercises): *The size of the company – it is growing. Its address and telephone number. The sort of company it is – a freight forwarder. It is a small friendly office. Mr G Davis is the assistant manager.*

Aim: Vocabulary development; for SS to learn more about Transworld.

The puzzle can be done in pairs or individually, in class or set as homework. Discussion about Transworld and the work of a freight forwarder can be in L1 in a monolingual class if preferred.

NB Transworld Freight is a public limited company, which is what the initials 'plc' in the name stand for. See Unit 10 for the differences between a private and a public limited company according to the most recent Companies Act of 1980. Incidentally, company names can take a singular or plural verb (eg Transworld is a plc; Transworld arrange transportation.)

Exercise 1.6 The alphabet (LD)

Answers: *1 BOCJ* *2 FBBD* *3 AELZ* *4 XMPG* *5 UVTT* *6 IHYR* *7 GGCB* *8 VTWE* *9 DIUF* *10 ENQS* *11 OKJG* *12 WUUW* (The tapescript for this exercise is not printed in the SB.)

Aim: Practice of the letters of the alphabet.

Revise the pronunciation of the letters of the alphabet with the SS before they do this exercise. Note that when a letter, for example G, is repeated, we say *double G*.

In number 12 notice the stress difference between the letter *W* (double-u: Ooo) and *double U* (ooO).

Ask SS to check their answers in small groups, which will give them practice in pronouncing the letters. Afterwards individuals from the groups can be asked to say the letters aloud to the class so that you have overall control of the corrections. The LD gives spelling practice.

You can give further practice in spelling and saying the letters of the alphabet by asking SS to spell words they have recently learned. This can be organised as a team game with SS from opposing teams giving each other words to spell.

If you ask SS to spell the sentence *The quick brown fox jumps over the lazy dog*, they will have to say every letter of the alphabet.

Exercise 1.7 Greetings and introductions

Answers: Informal dialogue: Susan: *John. It's lovely to see you.* John: 9. Susan: 5. John: 12. Susan: 2. Penny: 4. John: *Hallo, Penny. Nice to meet you.*
Formal dialogue: Susan Smith: *Good afternoon. Can I help you?* John Jones: 6. Susan Smith: 3. JJ: 11. SS: 10. Miss Brown: 13. JJ: *How do you do, Miss Brown.*

Aim: Revision of informal and formal greetings and introductions.

This exercise can be done individually or in pairs in class or prepared for homework. To check the exercise, ask SS to say the dialogue aloud working in pairs.

Exercise 1.8 Greeting and introducing people

Aim: Practice of formal and informal greetings and introductions.

Follow the instructions in the SB. Make sure the SS are very clear about what to do before the whole class starts moving around (see note on whole class activities, TB pages xx–xxi).

Exercise 1.9 Requests (LD A & B)

Answers: *See LDT*

Aim: Practice of polite requests and the *will* future to show an immediate decision.

Prepare this exercise by teaching the *could you* and *will* forms and getting SS to ask one another to do things in the classroom, such as: open the window, close the door, give somebody a book etc. Before SS do the exercise in closed pairs, prepare it T–S and in open pairs (see TB introduction pages xvii–xix). Note that today it is common to use *will* for all persons although some people still prefer to use *shall* in the first person singular and plural.

Exercise 1.10 Telephone enquiries

Answers: *1 Good morning 2 advert 3 I'd like 4 job 5 Could you 6 a bit more 7 the job and company 8 pay 9 I'll expect to hear 10 soon 11 Goodbye.*

Aim: Understanding words from context; linking the oral and written forms of English words.

Ask SS to read quickly through the exercise and suggest words to fill the gaps. Then play the tape as many times as necessary for them to write down the missing words. Ask them to write down the name 'Geoffries' which occurs at the end of the dialogue, because it practises again recognition of the alphabet.

Ask SS to learn this dialogue for homework as it will be used as the basis of further dialogues in the following exercises (see the notes on presenting dialogues in TB introduction page xix).

Exercise 1.11 Guided dialogue

Aim: Oral practice of telephone enquiries.

Look at the advertisement in Exercise 1.3 and discuss with SS the changes they will make from the dialogue in the previous exercise. SS can then do the exercise in open or closed pairs.

Exercise 1.12 Business letter terminology

Answers: The numbers in Exercise 1.10 correspond to the following words in the business letter: *1 Dear Mr Davis 2 advertisement 3 I would like 4 position 5 I would be grateful if you could 6 further information 7 working conditions 8 salary 9 I look forward to hearing 10 in the near future 11 Yours sincerely*

Aim: Comparison of oral and written forms.

SS should be able to do this exercise without preparation. Ask them to work individually or in pairs in class or set the exercise for homework.

Ask the SS to suggest (possibly in L1) differences between spoken and written language, eg the use of punctuation, capital letters, pronunciation, the use of contractions such as *I'd* for *I would* in spoken language and preference for the full form in written language, the use of abbreviations in spoken language, hesitation and repetition and the fact that sentences frequently are not completed in spoken language etc. This should help reinforce their accuracy in written work, help their listening comprehension and encourage their fluency in spoken English.

Exercise 1.13 Formal written style

Answers: *1 I look forward to seeing you next week.* *2 I would be grateful if you could give me some information about the job.* *3 I would be grateful if you could send me your price list.* *4 I look forward to receiving the application form in the near future.* *5 I would be grateful if you could see me this week.* *6 I look forward to meeting you at the conference.*

Aim: Practice of two commonly used business letter phrases.

SS should be able to do this exercise either in class or for homework without preparation. Ask them to find the two phrases in the business letter in Exercise 1.12 to use as a model.

Exercise 1.14 A letter of enquiry

Answer: Sample letter:

Student's address

Personnel Manager
Transworld Freight plc
74 Dockside
Manchester M15 7BJ

Date

Dear Sir or Madam

I saw your advertisement for a Senior Accounts Clerk in the Morning Sun of (recent date) and I would like to apply for the job.

I would be grateful if you could send me an application form and further information about the salary and working conditions.

I look forward to hearing from you in the near future.

Yours faithfully

Student's signature

Student's name and title

Aim: Practice of the format and conventions in a business letter and specifically in writing a letter of enquiry.

SS can use the business letter in Exercise 1.12 as a model for this letter. You can also refer them to the notes in the SB on business letter format and convention at the end of this unit. Discuss the layout and convention of business letters when you have given back their corrected letters. Elicit from them *why* they think the layout and conventions are as they are (this will help them remember):

- The writer's address is at the top of the letter so that the reader knows where to write back to; companies usually have this address printed to save secretaries time.
- Companies keep a record of each letter for future reference, so the reader's name and address is written on the letter. This also means that if the letter is mislaid in the reader's company, anyone who finds it knows who to give it back to – particularly if the reader has left the firm, but the person who now has that job still needs the letter.
- The date tells you when the letter was written, so that you know whether it was before or after other events; similarly you should always refer to the date of previous correspondence in a letter to help your reader know what you are talking about.
- Parts of the letter are usually in the same place, so that you know where to look for the information you want.
- A minimum of punctuation is used in the headings and endings of letters to save the typists' time, but punctuation is used in the body of the letter because it affects the meaning of sentences.
- Block style is more common, because it is quicker to use on a typewriter or word processor. And saving time saves money. Note that if SS use block style in handwritten letters, they should leave a line space between paragraphs so that it is clear where paragraphs begin and end.
- Print your name after your signature because signatures are notoriously hard to read.
- Write your title before or after your name, so that the reader knows how to reply to you: *Mr* for a man, *Mrs* for a married woman, *Miss* for an unmarried woman, *Ms* for a woman when you do not know whether she is married or not (NB there is some controversy about the use of *Ms* which is linked in some people's minds with the feminist movement).

Although they do not occur in this letter, the following points may also be useful:

- When the letter is written by someone representing a firm, that person's position in the company should be written under his/her name at the bottom of the letter.
- Many firms have a system of reference for easy recognition of letters, eg *Our ref: GA/dg*
  Your ref: 006354

In this case *GA* probably stands for the name of the writer (Geoffrey Andrews) and *dg* for the typist (*Diana Green*). The other reference is probably an order or invoice number. The references usually go above the opening salutation.

- If anything is enclosed with the letter (eg an application form) the letters *Enc* or *Encl* are written at the bottom of the letter to remind the person who sends the letter to put it in the envelope and the person who opens the letter to take it out.
- If someone (eg a secretary) signs the letter on behalf of the writer, or an employee signs on behalf of a company, that person puts the letters *pp* (per procurationem) in front of the writer's or company's name. (See also use of *pp* on air waybill on SB p 91.)

Note that each company has its own style for writing business letters so SS should expect to see variations on these suggestions. However, these notes are acceptable in the modern business world and the important thing is that SS concentrate on learning to *produce* one form correctly.

NB Information about British and American addresses is given in WB Exercise 1a. WB Exercises 1b, 1c and 1d give further practice in job applications. See also notes about controversial parts of business letters in TB after Exercise 8.12. Do not try to cover all these points at once. Revise what you have already done and add more information when you do exercises on business letters, eg Exercises 2.12 and 8.12.

LABORATORY DRILLS TAPESCRIPT

Drill 1.1

Say the past tense of these regular and irregular verbs, like this:

P: Do
R: *Did*

Now you try.

P: Handle
R: *Handled*
P: Talk
R: *Talked*
P: Spend
R: *Spent*
P: Deal
R: *Dealt*
P: Introduce
R: *Introduced*
P: Drink
R: *Drank*
P: Send
R: *Sent*
P: *Work*
R: *Worked*
P: Take
R: *Took*
P: Sit
R: *Sat*
P: Welcome
R: *Welcomed*
P: Eat
R: *Ate*/et/
P: Arrange
R: *Arranged*
P: Type
R: *Typed*

Aim: Practice of the form of the past simple of some regular and irregular verbs

Drill 1.2A

Listen to these statements and ask for more information, like this:

P: Nick's sitting at a table.
R: *Oh? What's he doing exactly?*

P: He's typing a letter. Sandra works in reception.
R: *Oh? What does she do exactly?*
P: Oh, she welcomes visitors.

Now you try.

P: Kevin works in the export department.
R: *Oh? What does he do exactly?*
P: He arranges exports. Oh look, that's Jane over there with Kevin.
R: *Oh? What's she doing exactly?*
P: I think she's just talking to him. She spends a lot of time at the airport.
R: *Oh? What does she do exactly?*
P: She handles all the airfreight. And this is David, who's dealing with customers' accounts.
R: *Oh? What's he doing exactly?*
P: I think he's sending out invoices. What *are* you doing, David?

Aim: Practice of the present simple and present progressive question forms and the pronouns *he/she*

Drill 1.2B

Talk about people's jobs. Say these sentences in the present simple tense, like this:

P: She handled airfreight.
R: *She handles airfreight.*

Now you try.

P: We worked for Transworld.
R: *We work for Transworld.*
P: I dealt with customers' accounts.
R: *I deal with customers' accounts.*
P: She typed letters.
R: *She types letters.*
P: They took shorthand.
R: *They take shorthand.*
P: He did the filing.
R: *He does the filing.*
P: He arranged exports.
R: *He arranges exports.*

Aim: Practice of the form of the present simple tense

Drill 1.2C

Talk about what people are doing now. Say these sentences in the present progressive tense, like this:

P: He sat at a table.
R: *At the moment he's sitting at a table.*

Now you try.

P: She welcomed David.
R: *At the moment she's welcoming David.*
P: He talked to Jane.
R: *At the moment he's talking to Jane.*
P: She typed a letter.
R: *At the moment she's typing a letter.*
P: He did the filing.
R: *At the moment he's doing the filing.*
P: He ate a sandwich.
R: *At the moment he's eating a sandwich.*

Aim: Practice of the form of the present progressive tense

Drill 1.6

Spell these words, like this:

P: Customs
R: *CUSTOMS*

Now you try.

P: Arrange
R: *A double RANGE*
P: Dealt
R: *DEALT*
P: Freight
R: *FREIGHT*
P: Accounts
R: *A double COUNTS*
P: Export
R: *EXPORT*
P: Ate
R: *ATE*
P: Handle
R: *HANDLE*

Aim: Spelling practice and practice of the pronunciation of letters of the alphabet

Drill 1.9A

Reply to these requests, like this:

P: Could you send a price list please?
R: *I'll send it at once.*

Now you try.

P: Could you reply as soon as possible please?
R: *I'll reply at once.*
P: Could you ring Mr Andrews please?
R: *I'll ring him at once.*
P: Could you copy the report please?
R: *I'll copy it at once.*
P: Could you type the memo please?
R: *I'll type it at once.*
P: Could you file the correspondence please?
R: *I'll file it at once.*
P: Could you answer the letter please?
R: *I'll answer it at once.*

Aim: Practice of the *will* form used for an immediate decision about the future

Drill 1.9B

Make requests, like this:

P: Send a price list
R: *Could you send a price list please?*

Now you try.

P: Reply as soon as possible
R: *Could you reply as soon as possible please?*
P: Ring Mr Andrews
R: *Could you ring Mr Andrews please?*
P: Copy the report
R: *Could you copy the report please?*
P: Type the memo
R: *Could you type the memo please?*
P: File the correspondence
R: *Could you file the correspondence please?*
P: Answer the letter
R: *Could you answer the letter please?*

Aim: Practice of polite requests

WORKBOOK ANSWERS

Exercise 1a Addresses

1 *Mr C Faram*
Millco Ltd
The Mills
River Street
Halifax HX5 7PT
England

2 *Ms A Egler*
Vice President
Computerco Inc
6355 Beacon Street
Fairfax
Virginia 22031
USA

3 *Ms Elizabeth Shepherd*
Senior Accounts Clerk
Transworld Freight plc
74 Dockside
Manchester M15 7BJ

4 *Mr G Dumiticz*
Sampson Silks
22 Main Street
Pittsburgh
Pennsylvania 15217

Exercise 1b A letter of application

62 Longford Lane
London EC4 7EL

Personnel Manager
Whitehouse & Co Ltd
69 Puritan Street
London WC2B 3XP

10 March 1983

Dear Sir or Madam

I enclose an application form for the position of Person Friday. As you can see, I do not have any experience, but my examination results were good and I am very interested in fashion.

I am available for an interview at your convenience.

I look forward to hearing from you.

Yours faithfully

Tracy Davis

Tracy Davis (Miss)

Exercise 1c Comprehension

1–c *2–b* *3–a* *4–b* *5–b*

Exercise 1d An application form

Whitehouse & Co Ltd, 69 Puritan Street, London WC2B 3XP

PLEASE COMPLETE IN BLOCK CAPITALS

APPLICATION FOR THE POSITION OF PERSON FRIDAY

Surname DAVIS First name(s) TRACY

Marital status SINGLE Telephone

Address 62 LONGFORD LANE, LONDON EC4 7EL

References:

Signature Tracy Davis Date 10 March 1983

NB After SS have done the exercise, check that they obeyed the instruction to 'write in block capitals'.

Exercise 1e Connections

a–f *b–i* *c–k* *d–j* *e–l* *g–m* *h–n*

NB Although phonetic script is sometimes used in the TB, it is not used very much in the SB. However, this was thought to be the only way of making the pronunciation of the alphabet (see the language notes to this unit) and some of the differences between British and American pronunciation.

UNIT TWO
BUYING AND SELLING
2

Language:	Sums of money
	Adjectives: *too short, not long enough*
	Collective nouns
	Count and mass nouns
	Question practice
Business/Commerce:	Receipts
	The vocabulary of buying and selling
	Cheques
	Memoranda
	Business letter format and conventions
	A simulation: Buying and selling

TEACHING NOTES

Exercise 2.1 Listening comprehension

Answers: *1–b* *2–b* *3–c* *4–c* *5–c* *6–b*

Aim: Listening comprehension.

Ask the SS a few questions to set the scene for this exercise before they listen to the tape, but do not pre-teach any of the vocabulary. Play the tape through twice if necessary and let SS compare their answers in pairs before you correct them.

Further exploitation of this exercise would be for SS to learn the dialogue on page 10 in preparation for Exercise 2.9 (see TB note for this exercise).

Exercise 2.2 Receipts

Answers: *a–20* *b–80p* *c–£16* *d–20*
e–80p *f–£16* *g–20* *h–60p* *i–£12*
j–£44 *k–£4.40* *l–£39.60* *m–20* *n–15p*
o–£3 *p–6* *q–35p* *r–£2.10* *s–£44.70*

Aim: Listening for specific information.

Discuss with SS what a receipt is (proof that something has been received). Check some of the new vocabulary in this exercise by asking them questions such as: *What is the reference number of the plates?* (ref 67/BW) *Which word means 'how many'?* (quantity) *Which words mean the price of one?* (unit price) *What do you call the machine on which the sales assistant adds up the cost of goods?* (a till or a cash register) etc. Note that the sign @ means *at* in the phrase *discount @ 10%*. Play the tape twice for SS to take down the missing figures, but give them time before and after each playing to compare the two receipts and think about which figure goes where. To check the exercise, let the SS say the figures to have practice in saying sums of money.

A simple transaction has been chosen deliberately to illustrate the concepts underlying a purchase. SS using this book who are already at work in more sophisticated areas of business may need reassurance that this scenario is relevant to them.
NB In invoices in Britain there would usually be some mention of VAT which stands for *Value Added Tax*. This is a tax added to invoices for many goods and services (at present at the rate of 15%). However all mention of VAT has been left out of this book to avoid an unnecessary and purely local complication.

Exercise 2.3 Sums of money (LD)

Answers: *See LDT*

Aim: Practice in saying and writing sums of money.

SS should be able to do this exercise without help by using the two examples as a model. You may wish to do some straightforward revision of numbers before they do this exercise. Check the exercise orally.

Exercise 2.4 Buying and selling

Answers: *1 The unit price of the speakers was $110 (110 dollars). 2 Stereo Inc was the seller. 3 Nick was the buyer. 4 Nick was the customer. 5 Nick paid for the equipment in cash. 6 Nick spent $220. 7 The bill came to $220. 8 The assistant gave him $30 change. 9 Nick's purchase was two speakers. 10 Nick purchased two speakers. 11 The supplier was Stereo Inc. 12 Nick's proof of payment was the receipt.*

Aim: Vocabulary development.

Ask the SS to work in pairs to complete this exercise without pre-teaching any vocabulary. Then put SS in groups of four to compare their answers before you correct them orally.

Since this is very basic vocabulary, it is important that SS know it well. Make sure that you revise it frequently.

Exercise 2.5 A transaction (LD)

Answers: *See LDT*

Aim: Further practice of the vocabulary in Exercise 2.4.

One way of doing this exercise is to divide your class into teams. Each team prepares five or six questions about Anne's transaction. Individuals from one team ask individuals from other teams the questions. Teams get points for correct questions and correct answers.
NB See the note on the stressed words in the LDT.

Exercise 2.6 Opposites (LD A & B)

Answers: *See LDT*

Aim: Practice of adjectival phrases.

SS should already know these common adjectives. Check this by saying any of the adjectives and asking different people quickly round the class to give the opposites. Teach the two expressions *too short* and *not long enough* by putting two chairs back to back about a foot or so apart. Bridge the gap with a long book, ruler or stick. Then take that object away and pretend you are trying to bridge the gap with another object which is too short. Ask SS to suggest ways of expressing what is happening. If nobody knows these two expressions, teach them. Do the exercise fairly quickly in open pairs.

Exercise 2.7 Collective nouns; count and mass nouns

Answers: *A cutlery* *B crockery* *C stationery* *D furniture* *E equipment* *F correspondence* *1 much* *2 knives* *3 any* *4 some* *5 much* *6 were* *7 desks* *8 correspondence*

Aim: Revision of the difference between count and mass nouns.

SS should already know the difference between count and mass nouns, but there is a note about their use in the language notes. Let them do this exercise individually or in pairs in class or for homework.

Exercise 2.8 Cheques

Answers: *1 Liz Shepherd* *2 28 March 1983* *3 Anne Bell* *4 Transworld Freight plc* *5 Transworld Freight plc* *6 Counts Bank plc* *7 Liz Shepherd* *8 Anne Bell* *9 Anne Bell* *10 Liz Shepherd* *11 Transworld Freight plc* *12 No* *13 90.10.109* *14 Liz Shepherd's* *15 Account*

The questions that mean the same are 1, 7, 10 and 3, 8, 9.
NB The *drawer* is usually the person who makes out the cheque, but in this case Liz Shepherd is making out the cheque on behalf of Transworld Freight. (In a letter, she would write the abbreviation *pp* before her signature – see TB page 8.)

Aim: Introducing cheques, bank accounts and the related vocabulary.

Present all the information in this exercise orally to the class before they look at their books. Most countries have banks and bank accounts and you can discuss what SS already know about your local system. Introduce basic vocabulary such as *account* and *cheque* at this stage. Do not go into too many details. This first introduction has been kept deliberately simple, for example, the different sorts of account are not introduced until Unit 8.

Elicit from SS the information they think should be included in a cheque and build up a sample cheque on the blackboard.

Then ask SS to open their books and see if they have put in too much information or missed out any information by comparing their cheque with the one in Exercise 2.8. Do not pre-teach all the words in the questions, but give them the information that a word ending in *-er* usually refers to a person who does an action while a word ending in *-ee* is a person an action is done to. Use as an example the words *employer* and *employee*. Check the SS' answers orally.

Discuss with the SS (possibly in L1) why people use cheques rather than cash: Because some people are dishonest, it is safer to carry or send cheques which cannot easily be stolen, rather than cash which anyone can spend; also, if you need to buy something unexpectedly, your cheque book gives access to more money than you are likely to carry around with you; a cheque book also provides a record of where you have spent your money (each cheque has a *stub* or *counterfoil* on which you record the details).

The two vertical lines on the cheque mean that this is a *crossed cheque*. This means that the cheque cannot be exchanged for cash over the counter (except for drawing money out of your own account), but must be paid into a bank account. In case of fraud, the bank can then trace which account the money was paid into. Nowadays, most cheques are issued by the bank with an automatic crossing, however it is still possible to have *open cheques* (cheques without a crossing) which can be exchanged for cash by the payee. Anyone can make an open cheque into a crossed cheque by drawing the two vertical lines on. SS do not need this information at this stage, unless they specifically ask about it.

Exercise 2.9 A simulation: Buying and selling

If this is the first time you have done a simulation, it is important that you read the information in the introduction to this TB on page xxi. In particular, try to make sure that each S only looks at the information relevant to his or her own role.

Before you do this exercise, discuss with the SS the language used between shoppers and shop assistants. It would be helpful if they learnt and performed the introductory dialogue to this unit on SB page 10. They could then adapt this for use in the simulation. The other vocabulary which might need pre-teaching is the adjectives to describe the chairs in phrases such as *the blue one*, *the comfortable one without arms*, *the striped one* etc.

Exercise 2.10 More about cheques

It is important that SS understand this exercise. In particular the key words are *to postdate a cheque*, *to endorse a cheque*, the words *or order* and the word *negotiable*. These are important for understanding Bills of Lading and Bills of Exchange which are covered later in this book. Treat the exercise as a reading comprehension and ask SS your own questions. Make sure that you ask questions with short answers. SS should enjoy writing a cheque to one another. If preferred you can photocopy a cheque form so that they actually have something to fill in.

SS are given further opportunities to write cheques in WB Exercises 2a and 5b.
NB In some countries it is illegal to postdate a cheque, but not in Britain, although the banks do not like the practice and will not pay the money until the date on the cheque. Note that banks in Britain do not pay interest on current accounts.

Exercise 2.11 Word puzzle

Answers: *post-dated* *signature* *guarantee card* *endorse* *cheque* *drawer* *negotiable* *order* *payee* *account holder* *branch* *make out* *account* *1 = T* *2 = E* *3 = S* *4 = P* *5 = I* *6 = C* *7 = R* *8 = A* *9 = D* *10 = O* *11 = N* *12 = U* *13 = B* *14 = G* *15 = L* *16 = W* *17 = M* *18 = Q* *19 = K* *20 = H* *21 = Y*

Aim: Consolidation of vocabulary in this unit.

SS should be able to do this exercise without any preparation. If necessary, remind SS not to fill in the squares in their SB.

Exercise 2.12 Mistakes

Answers: *The position of the two addresses should be swapped over.*
A Bell's name should not be written at the top of the letter, it should go at the bottom under her signature in the form Miss Anne Bell *or* Anne Bell (Miss). *Under that should go her position in the company.*
There should be a post code after Manchester *in Transworld's address.*
You do not need the word England *in Household Designs' address.*
There should not be a full stop after Ltd *in Household Designs' address, or in A Bell's name (unless you are using punctuation throughout the heading and ending of the letter – see TB notes after Exercise 8.12).*
In the date, 24st *should be* 24th, *or simply* 24.
March *should have a capital letter.*
Dear Mr Jones *instead of* Dear Sirs.
No comma after the opening salutation (unless you also put one after the closing salutation).
Either use block style (the preferred style) and do not indent the first paragraph, or use the indented style and indent both paragraphs. With block style Yours sincerely *should also be on the left.*
The word supply *should not be broken at that point in the word – in order to avoid this kind of problem, tell SS never to break words at the end of a line (there are more important things to learn than the complicated rules about where you can break words).*

Aim: Consolidation of the layout and conventions of business letters (see Exercises 1.12 and 1.14).

Refer SS back to the language notes for Unit 1 to help them with this exercise. Revise information you covered then about the layout and conventions of business letters and add further information as necessary.

For additional practice, you could ask SS to write a reply to this letter.

As a class project, you could open a class bank using play money. Ask SS to open accounts and write cheques, pay money in and withdraw money etc and the SS who are 'bankers' should prepare statements at the end of a certain period. All transactions should be carried out in English. The bank could then be revived in Unit 8 when SS can have overdrafts, loans and deposit accounts.

LABORATORY DRILLS TAPESCRIPT

Drill 2.3

Say the sums of money from your book, like this:

P: Number 1
R: *Seventy-nine pounds, thirty pence*

Now you try.

P: Number 2
R: *Two hundred and fifty-three pounds*
P: Number 3
R: *Five hundred and sixty-nine dollars and fifty cents*
P: Number 4
R: *Sixty-four dollars and ninety-six cents*
P: Number 5
R: *Two dollars*
P: Number 6
R: *Two thousand, three hundred and eighty-seven pounds*
P: Number 7
R: *Eighty-five pounds, forty-one pence*
P: Number 8
R: *One thousand, two hundred pounds*
P: Number 9
R: *Seven hundred and ninety pounds, ninety pence*

Aim: Practice of numbers and in saying sums of money
NB The answers to 3, 4 and 5 are in an American accent.

Drill 2.5

Ask questions from these statements, like this:

P: Each knife cost *35 pence*
R: *How much did each knife cost?*

Now you try.

P: The unit price was *35 pence*.
R: *What was the unit price?*
P: The seller was *Household Designs*.
R: *Who was the seller?*
P: *Anne* was the buyer.
R: *Who was the buyer?*
P: *Anne* was the customer.
R: *Who was the customer?*
P: She paid *by cheque*.
R: *How did she pay?*
P: She spent *£44.70*.
R: *How much did she spend?*
P: The bill came to *£44.70*.
R: *How much did the bill come to?*

P: The assistant didn't give her *any* change.
R: *How much change did the assistant give her?*
P: Her purchases were *cutlery and crockery*.
R: *What were her purchases?*
P: *Household Designs* was the supplier.
R: *Who was the supplier?*
P: Anne's proof of payment was *a receipt*.
R: *What was Anne's proof of payment?*

Aim: Question practice with new vocabulary
NB The words in italics in the prompts are slightly stressed to guide SS to the correct questions.

Drill 2.6A

Use the opposites of these adjectives, like this:

P: It's too short.
R: *Oh I see. It's not long enough.*

Now you try.

P: It's too expensive.
R: *Oh I see. It's not cheap enough.*
P: It's too big.
R: *Oh I see. It's not small enough.*
P: It's too wide.
R: *Oh I see. It's not narrow enough.*
P: It's too noisy.
R: *Oh I see. It's not quiet enough.*
P: It's too heavy.
R: *Oh I see. It's not light enough.*

Aim: Practice of adjectives and their opposites with *enough*

Drill 2.6B

Use the opposites of these adjectives, like this:

P: It's not long enough.
R: *Oh I see. It's too short.*

Now you try.

P: It's not cheap enough.
R: *Oh I see. It's too expensive.*
P: It's not small enough.
R: *Oh I see. It's too big.*
P: It's not narrow enough.
R: *Oh I see. It's too wide.*
P: It's not quiet enough.
R: *Oh I see. It's too noisy.*
P: It's not light enough.
R: *Oh I see. It's too heavy.*

Aim: Further practice of adjectives and their opposites with *too*

WORKBOOK ANSWERS

Exercise 2a A cheque

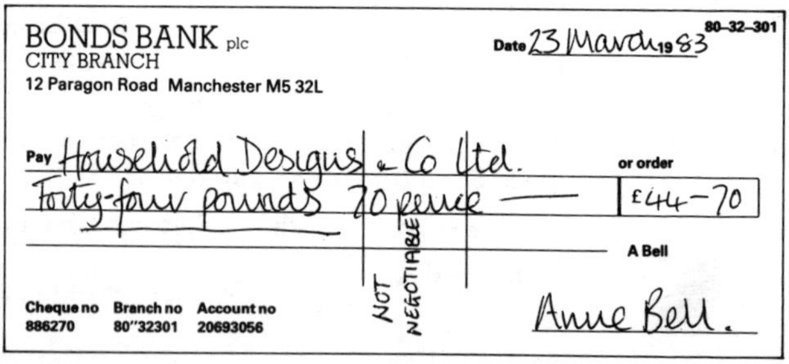

NB Where the amount of money is written in words, a line is often drawn in any remaining space to be certain that no extra writing can be fraudulently inserted.

Exercise 2b Prepositions

1 in cash 2 by cheque 3 come to 4 of the speakers 5 out

Exercise 2c Word order

1 I would like one of those. 2 That is much too expensive. 3 Could you show me the blue one please? 4 How much does the big one cost? 5 I can give you a ten per cent discount. 6 It is a very expensive calculator.

Exercise 2d Colours

beige, black, blue, brown, cream, green, grey, orange, pink, purple, red, white, yellow
1 = R, 2 = E, 3 = G, 4 = H, 5 = L, 6 = Y, 7 = B, 8 = U, 9 = P, 10 = M, 11 = C, 12 = D, 13 = W, 14 = A, 15 = O, 16 = N, 17 = T, 18 = I, 19 = K

Exercise 2e Punctuation in money

2b $22,222.22
3a £10,101,010,101 b £101,010,101.01
4a $1,765 b $17.65
5a £543,219,876 b £5,432,198.76
6a $1,000,000 b $10,000.00

UNIT THREE

TRANSPORTATION

3

Language:	Confirming question tags Dimensions *Used to do* Reported speech Comparatives Connectors Question practice
Business/Commerce:	Comparative methods of transportation Freight rates Containerisation Note-taking Oral (and written) presentation

TEACHING NOTES

Exercise 3.1 Listening comprehension

Answers: *a Weston* *b Easton* *c Beeton* *d Sutton* *e Norton* *f Ayton* *1 true* *2 true* *3 true* *4 true* *5 false* *6 true* *7 false* *8 true*

Aim: Listening comprehension.

Before you do this exercise, pre-teach the words in the key on the map by asking check questions such as, *When you travel by car do you go by road or by rail? What is a town on the coast where ships can visit called?* etc. SS do not have to understand every word of the conversation. The important thing is that they pick out the information they need.

A pair work exercise for further practice is the following:

P: *Beeton is on the coast, isn't it?*
R: *Yes it is./No it isn't actually.*

P: *There isn't an airport at Sutton is there?*
R: *No there isn't./Yes there is actually.*

Copy the intonation pattern from the tape when Nigel Storke said *Beeton's on the coast though, isn't it?*

Exercise 3.2 Transportation

Answers: *1 rate* *2 charge* *3 departure* *4 destination* *5 case* *6 pack* *7 volume* *8 measurements* *9 conventional* *10 cargo* *11 freight* *12 weight* *13 container* *14 standard* Hidden word: *transportation*

Aim: Presentation of commercial information/vocabulary; training SS to understand words from context.

Ask SS to do this exercise in pairs without any previous

preparation. The context, the clues and the puzzle should give them enough guidance to work out the answers by themselves. If necessary, remind SS not to write in their SBs. It is important that SS know this vocabulary, so revise it by asking check questions either at the end of the lesson or in a subsequent lesson. Note that *waggon* is spelt *wagon* – American English.

NB Conventional cargo (any goods in transit not in containers) can also be called *break bulk* cargo. You might also like to teach the word *capacity*. The *volume* of something is the three-dimensional space it takes up, the *capacity* of something is the amount it can hold inside it. So you can talk about the volume of a crate, the capacity of a lorry, but a container is thought of as having both volume and capacity. Which is the greater? (Volume, of course, because capacity is the volume minus the thickness of the container.)

Exercise 3.3 Questioning (LD)

Answers: *See LDT*

Aim: Question practice, reading comprehension and use of new vocabulary.

Do this exercise in open pairs round the class.

Exercise 3.4 Problem-solving

Answers: *1 £300 (Kevin must pay whichever rate is the greater) 2 £270 (£300–£30 discount) 3 Kevin's consignment would fit in a 20-foot container (see two alternative drawings below).*

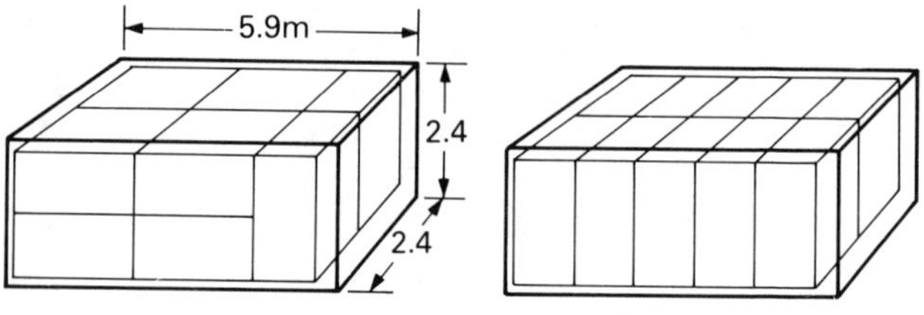

4 £50 (50p × 100K) You must take whichever price works out to be the greater (and 30 cu m × 50p = £15). 5 $5 (the price is the same whichever way you work it out: (5 tonnes × $1 or 10 m^3 × 50¢). 6a volume b weight c weight d volume 7 They might be different distances apart and be sent by different means of transport. 8 See Exercise 3.10.

Aim: To help SS understand how consignments are priced and to consider the use of containers.

Again ask SS to work in pairs or small groups. Working out these problems should help SS understand the practical considerations for sending goods in containers. Questions 7 and 8 demand that SS think for themselves. Question 8 is a preparation for the reading comprehension later in the unit.

NB Although Britain now officially uses metric measurements, containers are still frequently referred to as being 20-foot or 40-foot. When you talk about the capacity of a ship, you refer to its *TEUs* (*Twenty-foot Equivalent Units*), ie the number of 20-foot containers it can carry. The abbreviation FCL stands for *full container load* and LCL stands for *less than a container load*. When you are sending goods which are LCL, the freight forwarder tries to find other goods going to the same place to make up a FCL. Mixing different cargo in one container is known as *groupage*. Packing a container with goods is called *stuffing* it.

Exercise 3.5 Dimensions (LD)

Answers: *See LDT 1 80 square centimetres 2 75 cubic metres 3 2400 cubic centimetres 4 1.9 square metres 5 5.5 square kilometres 6 7,200 cubic centimetres 7 7 cubic kilometres 8 40 square kilometres*

Aim: Number practice.

Pre-teach *area* (of a plane) and *volume* (of a three-dimensional object) using pictures on the board (see below). This exercise can be given for written work and then checked orally in class.

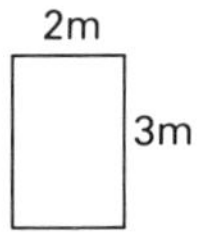

The size of this piece of paper is 2m by 3m. The area is (2m × 3m =) 6 square metres.

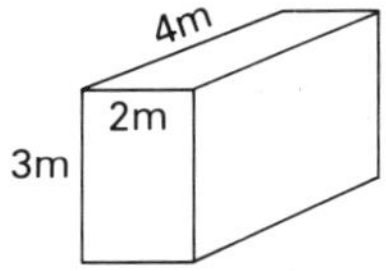

The dimensions of this box are 2m by 3m by 4m. Its volume is (2m × 3m × 4m =) 24 cubic metres.

Exercise 3.6 Used to do (LD)

Answers: *See LDT 1 They used to, but they don't now. 2 They didn't use (used) to, but they do now. 3 There used to be, but there isn't now. 4 He used to, but he doesn't now. 5 They didn't use to, but they do now. 6 They didn't use to, but they do now.*

Note that *used* in *used to do* is pronounced /ju:st/, but *used* in *I used the photocopier* is /ju:zd/.

Aim: Practice of the form and meaning of *used to*.

Pre-teach *used to*. You can either use examples which will be familiar to all the SS (eg changes in the local neighbourhood), or use the following situation:

Draw a picture of a man on the board. Describe his life with the following sentences: 1 *He eats in the best restaurants* (draw a plate on the blackboard). 2 *He has a fast car* (draw a car on the blackboard). 3 *He travels round the world* (draw a globe). How can he afford to do this? 4 *He steals diamonds* (draw diamonds on blackboard). Practise the four sentences in the present simple tense round the class by pointing at the pictures on the blackboard. Now explain that you are talking about last year. This year the man is in prison (draw bars over picture of man). Point to the previous pictures and ask the SS whether the man still does the same things. Elicit or teach the four sentences: *He used to eat well, but he doesn't now. He used to have a fast car, but he doesn't now* etc. Practise the four sentences round the class and then write them on the blackboard.

Establish the drill in this exercise as open pairs and then let SS work in closed pairs. Note that each exchange between two SS consists of three lines. Do not be tempted to use three different SS for the three different lines.

Exercise 3.7 Comparing (LD)

Answers: *See LDT*

Aim: Practice of comparatives.

SS will probably already know these comparatives and the vocabulary should be clear from the pictures. However, you may need to pre-teach *trailer*. The exercise is best done in open pairs round the class. More comparisons are possible than appear in the laboratory drill.
WB Exercise 3b consolidates SS' knowledge of the different means of transport.

Exercise 3.8 Sending a consignment

Answer: SS have a free choice of answer.

Aim: Further practice of comparatives in a freer situation.

Ask SS to agree with a partner which method of transportation is best. Ask SS to justify their decisions to the class. Only correct mistakes in the use of comparatives and superlatives.

Exercise 3.9 Reported speech and used to do (LD A & B)

Answers: *See LDT*

Aim: Practice of reported speech and further practice of *used to*.

Remind SS of the straightforward change from simple present to simple past in reported speech where the verb of saying is in the past. They will probably already know this. Establish the form of the drill in open pairs and ask SS to do it in closed pairs.
WB Exercise 3a further practises reported speech in the past.
NB In LD B, the negative of sentences like *I think she works for BOS* is *I don't think she works for BOS* not *I think she doesn't . . .*

Exercise 3.10 Containerisation

Answers: *1 for example* *2 so* *3 but* *4 This is because* *5 also* *6 As a result* *7 because* *8 On the other hand* *9 Also*

Sample summary: *Many big ports today are containerised,*

because the handling of containers has many advantages over conventional cargo. It takes fewer men to handle containers than to load and unload conventional cargo, so it is quicker. This is because there is special loading equipment and there are special container carriers in all kinds of transport. At his place of business the exporter packs the goods into a container which is not opened till it arrives at its destination. As a result fewer goods are stolen or damaged. Wages bills are lower because you need fewer men to handle the goods. On the other hand more people are out of work. Also the special equipment for handling the containers is very expensive and most ports are still not specially adapted for container traffic.

Aim: Recognition of connectors; practice of summarising.

SS will already have met many of these connectors, but you could pre-teach the following: *John is very fat*←*He eats a lot.* Join with *because* or *This is because. John eats a lot*→*He is very fat.* Join with *so* or *As a result. John is very fat. Mary is very thin.* Join with *but* or *On the other hand. John is very fat. He is very tall.* Join with *also* (*He is also very tall.*)

Ask SS to decide on their own or in pairs which words they think will fill which gap in the exercise. Discuss (possibly in L1) which ideas the connectors join and what relationship they express between the ideas.

In class ask SS to suggest which words and phrases can be omitted from the summary. SS can write up their own version of the summary for homework.

Exercise 3.11 Note-taking

Answers: Conventional cargo advantages: *Fewer people out of work, no special equipment.* Disadvantages: *slower, more damage, more goods stolen, higher wages bills.* Containerised transport advantages: *quicker, lower wages bills, less damage, fewer goods stolen.* Disadvantages: *more unemployment, equipment very expensive.*

Sample sentences: *On the one hand conventional cargo needs no special equipment, but on the other hand wages bills are higher. Although the equipment is very expensive for containerised transport, more goods are stolen with conventional cargo. On the one hand there is less damage with containerised transport, but on the other hand the equipment is very expensive.*

Aim: Reading comprehension, note-taking and practice of comparatives.

Having summarised the passage, SS are now asked to reduce it even further. When taking notes of this kind, ask SS to decide which words contain the essential meaning. Looking at it from the other point of view, the words that are omitted are the same words that are omitted from telexes (see Exercise 11.10).

SS can prepare their notes in class or for homework (if necessary, remind them not to write in their books), and they can be checked orally in class using the suggested format. Note that both the phrases compare two contrasting ideas.

Exercise 3.12 Oral (and written) presentation

Aim: To introduce SS to ways of presenting information clearly in oral and written form.

Take suggestions from the SS and build up on the blackboard a paragraph about the disadvantages of containerised transport. Then play the tape and ask SS to compare their version with the taped version. Note that although the taped version is clear it is slightly more repetitious than a written summary. Give SS the chance to prepare their talks on the three subjects for homework, but do not let them read from a prepared talk in class. (See also note in TB introduction pages xxi–xxii.)

LABORATORY DRILLS TAPESCRIPT

Drill 3.3

Ask questions, like this:

P: Ask about the consignment
R: *What was the consignment?*

Now you try.

P: Ask about the number of cases.
R: *How many cases were there?* (What was the number of cases?)
P: Ask about the means of transport.
R: *What was the means of transport?*
P: Ask about the measurements of the cases.
R: *How big were the cases?* (What were the measurements of the cases?)
P: Ask about the volume of each case.
R: *What was the volume of each case?*
P: Ask about the volume of the consignment.
R: *What was the volume of the consignment?*
P: Ask about the weight of each case.
R: *How much did each case weigh?* (What was the weight of each case?)
P: Ask about the freight rate.
R: *How much was the freight rate?*
P: Ask about the weight of the consignment.
R: *How much did the consignment weigh?* (What was the weight of the consignment?)
P: Ask about the charge by volume.
R: *What was the charge by volume?*
P: Ask about the charge by weight.
R: *What was the charge by weight?*

Aim: Question practice with new vocabulary (Alternative questions which are also acceptable are given in brackets)

Drill 3.5

Say the dimensions, like this:

P: Number 1
R: *Sixteen by five centimetres*

Now you try.

P: Number 2
R: *Thirty by two point five by one metre*
P: Number 3
R: *Twenty by four by thirty centimetres*
P: Number 4
R: *Nineteen by nought point one metres*
P: Number 5
R: *One point one by five kilometres*
P: Number 6
R: *Sixty by twelve by ten centimetres*
P: Number 7
R: *Seven by one by one kilometre*
P: Number 8
R: *Twenty by two kilometres*

Aim: Number practice in dimensions
NB The normal stress in *kilometre* is Oooo /'kiləmi:tə/, but it can also be pronounced oOoo /ki'lomitə/.

Drill 3.6

Ask about the past, like this:

P: There isn't an airport at Ayton nowadays.
R: *Did there use to be an airport at Ayton then?*

Now you try.

P: She's only worked for GLM since the takeover.
R: *Didn't she use to work for GLM then?*
P: They don't handle dangerous cargoes since the accident.
R: *Did they use to handle dangerous cargoes then?*
P: Transworld send containerised goods nowadays.
R: *Didn't they use to send containerised goods then?*
P: There isn't a railway line between Dutton and Norton any more.
R: *Did there use to be a railway line between Dutton and Norton then?*
P: He doesn't export to Italy now.
R: *Did he use to export to Italy then?*
P: Transworld arrange airfreight consignments these days.
R: *Didn't they use to arrange airfreight consignments then?*
P: They make stereo equipment since they expanded.
R: *Didn't they use to make stereo equipment then?*

Aim: Practice of the positive and negative question forms of *used to*

Drill 3.7

Refer to the table and give short answers to these questions:

P: Is it quicker by sea than by air?
R: *No. It's slower.*

Now you try.

P: Are trains more frequent than trailers?
R: *No. They're less frequent.*
P: Is it more expensive by train than by plane?
R: *No. It's less expensive.**
P: Is it slower by train than by trailer?
R: *No. It's quicker.*
P: Is it cheaper by ship than by train?
R: *No. It's more expensive.*
P: Are ships more frequent than trains?
R: *No. They're less frequent.*

Aim: Practice of comparatives
* NB *Cheaper* is also acceptable as the opposite of *expensive*.

Drill 3.9A

Comment on John's out-of-date knowledge, like this:

P: John said there was an airport at Dutton.
R: *There used to be an airport at Dutton, but there isn't now.*

P: John said she didn't work for BOS.
R: *She didn't use to work for BOS, but she does now.*

Now you try.

P: John said they handled dangerous cargo.
R: *They used to handle dangerous cargo, but they don't now.*
P: John said they didn't send containerised goods.
R: *They didn't use to send containerised goods, but they do now.*
P: John said there was a railway line between Dutton and Freetown.
R: *There used to be a railway line between Dutton and Freetown, but there isn't now.*
P: John said he exported to Spain.
R: *He used to export to Spain, but he doesn't now.*
P: John said Transworld didn't arrange airfreight consignments.
R: *They didn't use to arrange airfreight consignments, but they do now.*
P: John said they didn't make computers.
R: *They didn't use to make computers, but they do now.*

Aim: Practice of the form of *used to* and infinitive in context

Drill 3.9B

Confirm these statements by giving John's opinion, like this:

P: I think there's an airport at Dutton.
R: *Yes. John said there was an airport at Dutton.*

P: I don't think she works for BOS.
R: *Yes. John said she didn't work for BOS.*

Now you try.

P: I think they handle dangerous cargo.
R: *Yes. John said they handled dangerous cargo.*
P: I don't think they send containerised goods.
R: *Yes. John said they didn't send containerised goods.*
P: I think there's a railway line between Dutton and Freetown.
R: *Yes. John said there was a railway line between Dutton and Freetown.*
P: I think he exports to Spain.
R: *Yes. John said he exported to Spain.*
P: I don't think Transworld arrange airfreight consignments.
R: *Yes. John said they didn't arrange airfreight consignments.*
P: I don't think they make computers.
R: *Yes. John said they didn't make computers.*

Aim: Practice of reported speech in the past
NB Use the previous drill (3.9A) as the model intonation for neutral sentences in reported speech, not the intonation in this drill.

WORKBOOK ANSWERS

Exercise 3a Reported speech

2 She said she would send the consignment by air. 3 He knew that the consignment weighed 500 kilos. 4 She said it was more expensive by sea. 5 They said 15 men took four days to load a ship. 6 We thought there would be more unemployment.

Exercise 3b Means of transport

1 train 2 trailer 3 air 4 road 5 ship 6 plane 7 sea 8 rail

Exercise 3c Spelling

3 destination (correct) 4 freight (incorrect) 5 consignment (incorrect) 6 volume (correct) 7 machinery (incorrect) 8 container (correct) 9 discount (correct) 10 dimensions (incorrect)

Exercise 3d A puzzle

Take one piece of cutlery out of the box marked 'knives and forks'. Since you know the label is wrong, if you take out a fork you can put the label 'forks' on this box. If you take out a knife you can put the label 'knives' on this box. Put the label 'knives and forks' on the box which is still labelled and take that label and put it on the box which now remains unlabelled.

UNIT FOUR
INSURANCE

4

Language:	Roman numerals Years, centuries and dates Phrasal verbs
Business/Commerce:	Brief history of insurance and Lloyd's Insurance vocabulary and procedures Sorting and summarising correspondence relating to an insurance transaction Parts of a telex Standard business letter phrases: *I am pleased/sorry to inform you that...* A simulation: Broking and underwriting

TEACHING NOTES

Exercise 4.1 Listening comprehension

Answers: The picture sequence is *1, 2, 6, 3, 5, 4*. The dates are *6–a, 3–b, 5–c, 4–d*. *1 true* *2 true* *3 true* *4 true* *5 false* *6 false*

Aim: Listening comprehension; presentation of commercial information/vocabulary.

Pre-teach the words *insurance* and *to insure* and introduce the subject by asking SS to suggest from their own experience things that can be insured and things that you can insure against (you can insure property, your car, or yourself); you can insure against things like fire, theft, accidental damage, or liability (doing damage to other people).

Look at the pictures on SB page 29 and ask the SS to try to put pictures three to six in the right order from the clues in the pictures and captions. Then listen to the tape as confirmation of their answers. If necessary listen to the tape again to do the true/false questions.
NB Note that Lloyd's is an insurance *market*, not an insurance company. Different underwriters go there to sell insurance in their own right, Lloyd's itself does not sell insurance. Note also that Lloyds (spelt *without* an apostrophe) is the name of a major clearing bank in Britain.

Exercise 4.2 Roman numerals (LD)

Answers: *Odd numbers a–3, d–9, j–11, e–17, h–19 Even numbers k–2, g–4, c–6, l–10, i–12, f–14, b–20*

Aim: Number practice and introduction to roman numerals.

It is worth the SS learning the roman numerals up to 20 because they are frequently used for sub-sections in commercial reports and documents. On the blackboard show SS how the roman numerals are made up. I (1), II (2), III (3). V equals 5, so IV (one from five) equals 4, 6 equals V plus I (VI), 7 equals V plus II (VII) etc. The next critical number is 10 which is X, so 9 is I from X (IX) and 11 equals X plus I (XI) etc. Make sure you are practising the English numbers at the same time.

The other concept to teach is the difference between odd and even numbers. After that, SS can be left to do this exercise on their own or for homework.
The LD gives further practice of roman numerals.

Exercise 4.3 Years and centuries (LD A & B)

Answers: *See LDT*

Aim: Practice of years and ordinal numbers.

This can be done as a written exercise and checked orally in class. Note that in (h) BC stands for *before Christ*. 25BC is in the 24th century BC. The other dates are AD (*anno domini*, Latin for *the year of our Lord*).
NB Since various number forms are practised in this unit, it might be appropriate to do a mixed number dictation.

Exercise 4.4 Dates (LD A & B)

Answers: *See LDT*

Aim: Practice of ordinal numbers in dates; practice of the difference between British and American dates.

The SS will almost certainly know the months and dates already, but the important things to stress are (a) the difference between the way the British and American dates are said and (b) the difference between the way British dates are said and the way they are written, ie we say *the 6th of December*, but we write *6th December* or *6 December*. The exercise can be written or done orally.

Make a point of revising dates, both American and British forms, whenever you meet them in correspondence.
NB Although SS should know the ordinal numbers, it is perfectly acceptable to omit the ordinal abbreviations in business letters, which is then one less area for error in examinations.

Exercise 4.5 Insurance

Answers: *1 cover–iv, 2 proposal form–v, 3 broker–i, 4 underwriter–vii, 5 premium–iii, 6 claim–x, 7 compensation–ix, 8 insurance company–vi, 9 small print–viii, 10 policy/insurance certificate–ii*

Aim: Presentation of insurance vocabulary, guessing the meaning of words from context.

Read through the passage with the class without looking at the words below. Each time you reach a gap ask SS to suggest the sort of word or the meaning of the word which will fill the gap. For example, ask questions such as *Is it a person, a company, or a piece of paper? What is it used for?* etc. From this SS can decide what the words mean from the list on the right. Some of the words they will already know from the introductory dialogue (*broker, underwriter, insurance company*), but they can look up the others in the dictionary.

An alternative presentation, when you have established the meaning of the words from context, is the following. Without letting anyone else in the class hear, tell one S that the first word is *cover*, another S the second word is *proposal form*, the third S the third word is *broker* etc until each word is known by one person in the class. Then ask everybody to stand up and each person who knows one of the words can tell it to other people on a one-to-one basis. All the people who now know words can tell them to other people while at the same time trying to complete the rest of their own words. When any S has completed all the ten words he/she should sit down. Other SS then know that they can ask people sitting down for the remaining words they need. The activity should not take more than five minutes. (See note on the whole class activities on TB pages xx–xxi.)

For revision, you can write the eleven words on the board and ask check questions like those in the list in Exercise 5.4, eg *Which ones are people? Which two mean exactly the same thing? Which ones are to do with money?* etc.

Exercise 4.6 Phrasal verbs (LD)

Answers: *See LDT*

Aim: Introduction of the use of phrasal verbs with pronouns.

Although SS may not know all the more formal verbs in these sentences, they will probably know most of the phrasal verbs. They should work out which phrasal verb replaces which formal verb (if necessary with the help of a dictionary) before they do the next bit of the exercise. Show with the help of the following diagram how the word order changes when a pronoun is used with the phrasal verb.

it

I'm going to take out [insurance cover].

Do the exercise in open pairs in class. SS can write the exercise for homework.

NB You can *fill in* or *fill out* a form. The two phrasal verbs mean exactly the same in this case.

Exercise 4.7 Correspondence

Answers: *1–l 2–e 3–b 4–m 5–a 6–k 7–f 8–c 9–j 10–n 11–i 12–g 13–p 14–h 15–d 16–o*. The order of the letters is *iii–vi–ii–v–viii–vii–iv–i.*

Aim: Reading comprehension, skimming/scanning practice; consolidation of insurance procedures.

Do not pre-teach any unknown vocabulary in this exercise. The important thing is that SS can understand the message, not that they know all the words and structures. Do the exercise in class, preferably with SS working in pairs, and only give them a set amount of time in which to do it, probably about fifteen minutes. Check their answers orally in class for further practice of dates. Discuss with them how they know that different items of correspondence come before or after others. This is a test both of their knowledge of English and of their understanding of insurance procedures.

You could further exploit the correspondence by asking questions about the conventions, eg *Why is the closing salutation 'Yours faithfully' in letter 1? What do you think the references NS/Jl and 67/325708 stand for?* etc.

Exercise 4.8 Summarising correspondence

Answers: *Mr Perez has rung asking you to arrange insurance for a consignment to Madrid. Nigel Storke has written asking you to arrange insurance for a consignment to Madrid. Geoffrey Cook has written saying he will insure your shipment at 2 per cent. Mr Storke has telexed saying he has arranged insurance at 2 per cent. Mr Storke has written enclosing a cheque for the premium. Mr Cook has written enclosing your insurance certificate. Mr Perez has telexed asking you to claim for two damaged cases. Mr Storke has written asking you to arrange compensation for two damaged cases.*

Aim: Practice of the present perfect and guidance in summarising.

This exercise can either be written or done orally in class. SS should not need preparation.

xercise 4.9 Parts of a telex

Answers: *1 MADRID IMP 62502S 2 6.9.83 1420 3 ATTN 4 TWO CASES DAMAGED etc to . . . REPORT FOLLOWS 5 REGARDS*

Aim: Introduction to the parts of a telex.

To help the SS with this exercise, ask questions beforehand or afterwards to focus attention on the parts of a telex. ATTN stands for *attention*, or *'for the attention of'* and 1420 is the time on the twenty-four-hour clock. Ask SS which word is spelt wrongly (FOLLOWS/FOLLWS). Discuss with or elicit from the SS why parts of a telex are as they are: You dial your own code at the beginning of the telex to open a line. You then dial the code for the person you want to speak to and wait until the connection is established. You record the date and time for future reference. The message is in a reduced form to save money. At the end of the telex you type and wait for the two codes again to confirm that the telex connection has not been broken during the message. (See Unit 11 for telex abbreviations.)

Exercise 4.10 Giving information in letters

Answers: *1 I am sorry to inform you that the consignment was damaged.* *2 I am pleased to inform you that we will pay the compensation in full.* *3 I am sorry to inform you that your insurance policy is out of date.* *4 I am sorry to inform you that the goods were stolen.* *5 I am sorry to inform you that the ship arrived late.* *6 I am pleased to inform you that we are placing an order with you.*

Aim: Practice of a standard business letter phrase.

SS should be able to do this written exercise in class or for homework with no preparation.

Exercise 4.11 A simulation: Broking and underwriting

See note on simulations on TB page xxi.

For your initial preparation treat this exercise as a reading comprehension. Ask SS to read it through and then ask them check questions. Divide the class into two, half as brokers and half underwriters. Ask the brokers to prepare their brokers slips (they will not of course be able to fill in the premium rate until they have talked to the underwriters). At the same time each underwriter can be deciding on a premium rate. This premium rate can change in the course of the activity. Warn SS to keep a record of all their own transactions. Discuss with the SS the sort of language they will use, eg *Will you insure a consignment to Sidney? What premium rate will you charge me?* During the actual market ask all the underwriters to remain seated and ask the brokers to move around between underwriters. Give SS a five-minute warning before you stop the activity. End the activity by pretending to ring the Lutine bell, and announce that the New York Express en route from New York to Alexandria has sunk. All hands were saved, but all cargo was lost. (*Hands* is a way of referring to the people on board.) Ask the SS to sit down and work out how much money they have won or lost.

A 'broker's' example: He/she insures half the cargo (£2,500) at 1.5 per cent (£37.50) and half for 2 per cent (£50). The total premium, therefore, is £87.50. An 'underwriter' might insure four half cargoes of £2,500 @ 1.5 per cent (4 × £37.50 = £150) another might only insure a half cargo @ 2½ per cent and another @ 2 per cent making a total premium of £112.50

(£50 + £62.50). Check your SS' arithmetic – the total premiums received by the underwriters should be the same amount as the total paid by the brokers.
NB *IOU* represents the phrase *I owe you*. The symbol @ stands for *at*.

Exercise 4.12 Vocabulary puzzle

Answers: *1 fire brigade* *2 marine* *3 brokers* *4 century* *5 property* *6 trade* *7 underwriters* *8 cover* *9 premium*
Hidden word: *insurance*

Aim: Revision of vocabulary from this unit.

SS can do this exercise without preparation.

LABORATORY DRILLS TAPESCRIPT

Drill 4.2

Say the Roman numeral equivalent of these numbers, like this:

P: Fourteen
R: *XIV*

Now you try.

P: Ten
R: *X*
P: Three
R: *III*
P: Five
R: *V*
P: Six
R: *VI*
P: Twenty
R: *XX*
P: Fifteen
R: *XV*
P: Nine
R: *IX*
P: Four
R: *IV*
P: Eight
R: *VIII*
P: Eighteen
R: *XVIII*

Aim: Practice of numbers, Roman numerals and the pronunciation of the three letters *X*, *V* and *I*

Drill 4.3A

Say which century these years are in, like this:

P: Sixteen sixty-six
R: *That's in the seventeenth century.*

Now you try.

P: Nineteen fifty-two
R: *That's in the twentieth century.*
P: Two thousand
R: *That's in the twenty-first century.*
P: Eighteen seventy-four
R: *That's in the nineteenth century.*
P: Seventeen thirty-nine
R: *That's in the eighteenth century.*
P: Twelve twenty-five
R: *That's in the thirteenth century.*
P: Nineteen eighty-three
R: *That's in the twentieth century.*
P: Twenty-five BC
R: *That's in the twenty-fourth century BC*

Aim: Recognition of years and practice of ordinal numbers in centuries

Drill 4.3B

Say the years from the book, like this:

P: a
R: *Sixteen sixty-six*

Now you try.

P: b
R: *Nineteen fifty-two*
P: c
R: *Two thousand*
P: d
R: *Eighteen seventy-four*
P: e
R: *Seventeen thirty-nine*
P: f
R: *Twelve twenty-five*
P: g
R: *Nineteen eighty-three*
P: h
R: *Twenty-five BC*

Aim: Practice in saying numbers and years

Drill 4.4A

Say these dates as if you were British, like this:

P: Six stroke twelve
R: *The sixth of December*

Now you try.

P: Eight stroke nine
R: *The eighth of September*
P: Three stroke seven
R: *The third of July*
P: Ten stroke two
R: *The tenth of February*
P: Eleven stroke one
R: *The eleventh of January*
P: Four stroke twelve
R: *The fourth of December*
P: Five stroke five
R: *The fifth of May*

Aim: Recognition of numbers and practice of ordinal numbers and months in the spoken British form of dates

Drill 4.4B

Say these dates as if you were American, like this:

P: Six stroke twelve
R: *June twelfth*

Now you try.

P: Eight stroke nine
R: *August ninth*
P: Three stroke seven
R: *March seventh*
P: Ten stroke two
R: *October second*
P: Eleven stroke one
R: *November first*
P: Four stroke twelve
R: *April twelfth*
P: Five stroke five
R: *May fifth*

Aim: Recognition of numbers and practice of ordinal numbers and months in the spoken American form of dates
NB This drill is in an American accent.

Drill 4.6

Offer to help the speaker, like this:

P: I'm going to take out insurance cover.
R: *Let me take it out for you.*

Now you try.

P: I'm going to put in a claim.
R: *Let me put it in for you.*
P: I'm going to take off the discount.
R: *Let me take it off for you.*
P: I'm going to fill in the form.
R: *Let me fill it in for you.*
P: I'm going to work out the premium.
R: *Let me work it out for you.*
P: I'm going to look up the word.
R: *Let me look it up for you.*
P: I'm going to turn off the photocopier.
R: *Let me turn it off for you.*

Aim: Practice of the word order when pronouns are used with phrasal verbs

WORKBOOK ANSWERS

Exercise 4a Petty cash and vouchers

CASH RECEIVED Dr			CASH PAID				ANALYSIS			
Date	Ledger No.	Amount	Date	Details	Voucher No.	TOTAL	Postage	Travel	Stationery	Sundries
1983 28 July	C/D	5·37								
"	CB	14·63								
			28 July	stamps	96	4·50	4·50			
			29	biscuits	97	51				51
			1 Aug	petty cash book	98	34			34	
			1	taxi	99	4·00		4·00		
			3	milk	100	44				44
			4	coffee + sugar	1	2·18				2·18
			5	drawing pins	2	44			44	
			5	milk	3	22				22
			8	sellotape	4	2·55			2·55	
			9	tea bags	5	1·10				1·10
					TOTAL	16·~~36~~ 28	4·50	4·00	3·33	4·45

Exercise 4b Number crossword

Across *b 1463 e 44 g 255 i 100*
Down *a 96 c 445 d 34 f 400 g 29 h 51*

Exercise 4c Contractions

1 I have 2 She has 3 He is 4 I will 5 I would 6 He did not 7 I am 8 does not

Exercise 4d A business letter

Our ref: 67 . . . *Your* ref: NS/jl . . . Thank *you* for *your* letter . . . *I* am pleased to inform *you* that *we* will insure *your* . . . *I* would be grateful if *you* could . . . return *it* to *me* as soon . . . so that *I/we* can . . . *I/we* look forward . . . from *you* in the . . . *Yours* sincerely

UNIT FIVE
SALES DOCUMENTATION

5

Language:	Immediate reported speech
	Reported speech in the past
	You/one
	Non-defining relative clauses
	Past perfect tense
Business/Commerce:	Telephone conversations
	Sales and transport documentation
	An invoice and an order
	A memorandum

TEACHING NOTES

Exercise 5.1 Immediate reported speech

Answers: *See SB tapescript*

Aim: Selective dictation.

Ask SS to describe the situation by looking at the pictures in the introductory dialogue. Play the tape and then ask check comprehension questions. Play the tape for a second time for the SS to take selective dictation.

The picture sequence only covers the initial part of the tape, *not* the commercial element.

Exercise 5.2 Reported speech in the past (LD)

Answers: *See LDT*

Aim: Revision of reported speech.

Since this exercise is revision, SS should be able to do it without any preparation. Refer them to the language notes in Unit 3 if necessary. It can be written or done orally.

Exercise 5.3 Telephoning

Sample answers: *a Good morning. Transworld here. b Could I speak to Graham Davis please? c I'm afraid he's in a meeting at the moment. d I'm afraid he's on another line at the moment. e Can I take a message? f Would you like to wait? g Will you ask Mr Davis to call me back please? h Could you tell Mr Davis I rang please? i No thank you. I'll call back later. j My name is . . . and my telephone number is . . . k That's . . . l Goodbye.*

Aim: Practice of common telephone language.

SS should already know relevant phrases and structures for doing this exercise. They can model their dialogue on the pictures in the introductory dialogue on page 38.

Ask SS to prepare a written version of one dialogue for homework, but in class the exercise should be done orally, first in open pairs and then in closed pairs.

Exercise 5.4 Sales documentation

Answers: *1 invoice, pro-forma invoice* *2 consignment note, air waybill, air consignment note, Bill of Lading, combined transport document* *3 air waybill, air consignment note* *4 order* *5 consignment note, air waybill, air consignment note, Bill of Lading, combined transport document* *6 order, consignment note, invoice, statement* *7 order, consignment note, pro-forma invoice/invoice* *8 order air waybill/air consignment note, invoice, statement*

Aim: Introduction of vocabulary and commercial procedures to do with sales.

This exercise can either be done as a reading comprehension, or you can present the information orally and ask the questions while SS have their books closed. As you explain each of the new italicised words, write them on the blackboard so SS can refer to them. SS can write the exercise for homework as a check.
WB Exercise 5c is about paying on a pro-forma invoice and WB Exercise 9c gives further examples of sales documents.
NB The word *indent* is sometimes used to mean an order from abroad. In the days when export and travel were less easy than they are today, Indent Houses were agents who bought goods abroad on behalf of their customers. The order used in an Indent House was known as an indent. This is now a very old-fashioned term.

Exercise 5.5 You

Answers: *3–a* *4–b* *5–b* *6–a* *7–b* *8–a*

Aim: Listening comprehension, presentation of *you*.

In English we frequently use the word *you* to refer to anyone in a particular situation rather than 'you the listener'. Explain this to the SS with the help of the first two examples in this exercise. Then play the tape and see if they can work out the remainder of the examples.
NB An alternative to using *you* is to use *one*, eg *When one travels by train one needs a ticket.* In everyday speech, however, *one* sounds rather affected. *You* is the more common form. You can also use the plural: When *people* travel by train, *they* need a ticket.

Exercise 5.6 Relative clauses

Answers: *1 GLM paid the pro-forma invoice, which showed what the goods cost, before they received the goods.* *2 Transworld received a statement, which showed all their transactions.* *3 Anne gave the invoice, which is a request for payment, to Liz in the accounts department. 4 Kevin asked for the Bill of Lading, which is the consignment note for goods sent by sea. 5 BOS usually send goods by rail with a consignment note, which is a receipt for goods in transit. 6 Jane made out the combined transport document, which is used for goods sent by more than one means of transport.*

Aim: Practice of relative clauses, revision of sales documentation.

The examples in this exercise show SS how relative clauses are used. The exercise demands that the SS also think about the meaning of the words being defined.
NB Do not confuse SS by introducing the concept of defining relative clauses (see Unit 12) at this stage.

Exercise 5.7 Past perfect tense (LD)

Answers: *See LDT*

Aim: Presentation of past perfect tense.

The seven simple sentences in this exercise relate to Anne's life. Write them out of order on the blackboard, eg *Anne went to secretarial college. Anne got a job with Transworld. Anne left school* etc. Using any two of the sentences, establish the order in which Anne did them and show SS how the past perfect tense is used with *before* and *after* (if necessary pre-teach *before* and *after* using the days of the week, months of the year, numbers etc). SS should already know the past participles of all the verbs in this exercise, but they may need reminding of the two past participles used for the verb *go* (*She's been to secretarial college and now she is somewhere else. She's gone to secretarial college and she's still there*). Ask the SS to guess the order of the seven sentences. Write the words *then*, *later*, *finally*, *after that* on the blackboard and ask SS to join the sentences using them. The words can be used in any order as long as *finally* is used before the last sentence. Then refer SS to the SB to compare their suggestions with the order in the book before they do this exercise as suggested in closed pairs.

Exercise 5.8 More about the past perfect (LD)

Answers: *See LDT*

Aim: Further practice of past perfect in context relating to commercial procedures and sales documentation.

Set this exercise for homework without preparation.

Exercise 5.9 An invoice

Answers: *1 = T*	*2 = R*	*3 = C*	*4 = Q*	*5 = P*	*6 = Y*
7 = L	*8 = E*	*9 = U*	*10 = N*	*11 = I*	*12 = B*
13 = A	*14 = O*	*15 = D*	*16 = M*	*17 = H*	*18 = F*

The words are: *quantity (qty), and (&), pound (£), number (no), limited (Ltd), company (Co), public limited company (plc), telephone (tel), per cent (%), reference (ref)*

Aim: Presentation of an invoice, revision of abbreviations and symbols.

It is important to practise the spoken form of these abbreviations and symbols, because SS can get no clue from the written form. The exercise can be done for homework or as pairwork in class before or after Exercise 5.10.

Exercise 5.10 Comprehension

Answers: *1 Household Designs & Co Ltd 2 Transworld Freight plc 3 5th April 1983 4 ten 5 £66.00 6 £660.00 7 £594.00 (£660 minus £66, which is the 10% discount) 8 0455/0004 (the invoice number)*

Aim: Comprehension of an invoice.

This exercise is best done orally in class, so that you can deal with queries as they arise. Note in particular that a calendar month lasts from one date in one month to the same date in the following month (eg 4th April to 4th May is one calendar month). Calendar months are therefore of different lengths according to the month of the year. Sometimes firms prefer to keep a standard length of time for payment such as 30 or 60 days. Note also that 05 and 04 are written in the date, because frequently dates are written by a computer which must leave a space (represented by 0) for any possible figure.

(Sample order: See Exercise 5.11, page 42.)

TRANSWORLD FREIGHT PLC

74 Dockside
Manchester M15 7BJ

Tel: 061 8537272
Telex: 668013

Cables/telegrams: TRANSWLD MANCHESTER

ORDER

Order no: 009762
Date: 23 March 1983
TO: Household Designs & Co Ltd
22 High Street
Manchester M1 2BL

Qty	Description	Unit price
5	chairs ref C299432B (blue)	£66
5	chairs ref C299432G (green)	£66

Deliveries accepted only against our official order.
Please quote order no & date.

Signed . . [signature] . . .
Purchasing Officer

Ask SS to say in simpler language 'please quote invoice number when submitting payment' (something like: *Please tell us the invoice number when you pay*). It is not important that they learn this phrase, merely that they recognise what it means.

Exercise 5.11 An order

Sample order: *See page 41.*

Aim: To help SS understand the meaning of an invoice and an order and how they are used.

Ask SS to prepare this exercise in pairs or small groups. Discuss their answers in class, and then ask them to draw the order for homework. SS should be able to surmise most of the information and invent the rest.

Exercise 5.12 A memorandum

Answer: The missing words are underlined.

MEMORANDUM

TO: All staff

FROM: Liz Shepherd, Senior <u>accounts clerk</u>

DATE: 11 <u>April 1983</u>

SUBJECT: <u>Official order forms</u>

<u>I</u> would be grateful if all staff could remember to use an official order form when they buy goods for the office.

We need the order, which is our proof that someone in the office ordered the goods, before we can <u>pay</u> the invoice. Please send a copy of each order <u>to</u> the accounts department.

Thank <u>you</u>.

Liz Shepherd

Aim: Reading comprehension and consolidation of the format of a memo.

This exercise can be done in class or for homework.

LABORATORY DRILLS TAPESCRIPT

Drill 5.2

Repeat Sandra's account of her telephone conversation as she told it to Graham Davis later, like this:

P: Liz says she's got an order for some furniture.

R: *Liz said she'd got an order for some furniture.*

Now you try.

P: Liz says she can't find the order.
R: *Liz said she couldn't find the order.*
P: Anne says she wrote a letter of order.
R: *Anne said she'd written a letter of order.*
P: Anne says she didn't send an order form.
R: *Anne said she hadn't sent an order form.*
P: Liz says she needs an order number.
R: *Liz said she needed an order number.*
P: Liz says she'll pay it.
R: *Liz said she'd pay it.*
P: Anne says she also bought some cutlery.
R: *Anne said she'd also bought some cutlery.*
P: Anne says she didn't use an official order.
R: *Anne said she hadn't used an official order.*
P: Anne says she paid by cheque.
R: *Anne said she'd paid by cheque.*
P: Anne says she got a receipt.
R: *Anne said she'd got a receipt.*
P: Liz says she's got the receipt.
R: *Liz said she'd got the receipt.*
P: She says it's all right.
R: *She said it was all right.*

Aim: Practice of tense changes in reported speech in the past

Drill 5.7

Answer these questions by giving the correct information, like this:

P: Had Anne left school before she passed her exams?
R: *No. She'd passed her exams before she left school.*
P: Did Anne pass her exams after she'd left school?
R: *No. She left school after she'd passed her exams.*

Now you try.
(The second example is not repeated)

P: Did Anne leave school after she'd been to secretarial college?
R: *No. She went to secretarial college after she'd left school.*
P: Had Anne worked in a bank before she went to secretarial college?
R: *No. She'd been to secretarial college before she worked in a bank.*
P: Did Anne work in a bank after she'd lived in London.
R: *No. She lived in London after she'd worked in a bank.*
P: Had Anne moved to Manchester before she lived in London?
R: *No. She'd lived in London before she moved to Manchester.*
P: Did Anne get a job with Transworld before she'd moved to Manchester?
R: *No. She'd moved to Manchester before she got a job with Transworld.*
P: Did Anne work in a bank after she'd moved to Manchester?
R: *No. She moved to Manchester after she'd worked in a bank.*

Aim: Practice of the past perfect tense with *before* and *after*

Drill 5.8

Decide which of these events happened before the other and combine the sentences using the past perfect, like this:

P: GLM sent the invoice.
GLM sent the goods.
R: *GLM sent the invoice after they'd sent the goods.*

Now you try.

P: BOS received the order.
BOS sent the goods.
R: *BOS sent the goods after they'd received the order.*
P: BOS sent the statement.
Transworld received the goods.
R: *BOS sent the statement after Transworld had received the goods.*

P: Anne received the goods.
Anne paid the pro-forma invoice.
R: *Anne received the goods after she'd paid the pro-forma invoice.*

P: Mr Perez received the goods by air.
Mr Perez sent an order.
R: *Mr Perez received the goods by air after he'd sent an order.*
P: Transworld received the statement.
Transworld paid BOS.
R: *Transworld paid BOS after they'd received the statement.*

P: Kevin received the order.
Kevin made out the Bill of Lading.
R: *Kevin made out the Bill of Lading after he'd received the order.*

Aim: Practice of the form and meaning of the past perfect tense

WORKBOOK ANSWERS

Exercise 5a Say and tell

2 said 3 tell 4 told 5 tell 6 says 7 tells 8 is telling 9 told

Exercise 5b Spelling

1 speak 2 receipt 3 premium 4 meet/meat 5 received
6 kilo 7 field 8 employee 9 please 10 marine
11 peace/piece 12 procedure

Exercise 5c A pro-forma invoice

Anne Bell is paying for the book against a pro-forma invoice which she is paying in advance. Therefore she cannot be enjoying the book already.

MAIL ORDER BOOK CO LTD — PRO-FORMA INVOICE

CUSTOMER'S NAME: MISS A BELL — NO: 0037821
AND ADDRESS: 69 Maple Road, Manchester M3 2BY — DATE: 11/08/83

Qty	Description	Unit price	Amount
1	Book 'Personal Finance'	£3-95	£3-95
	postage & packing		80p
Please make your cheque for the total amount payable to MOBC Ltd.		TOTAL	£4-75

BONDS BANK plc
CITY BRANCH
12 Paragon Road Manchester M5 32L

Date 18 August 1983 — 80-32-301

Pay MOBC Ltd — or order
Four pounds 75 pence — £4-75

A Bell

Anne Bell

Cheque no 886275 — Branch no 80"32301 — Account no 20693056

CONSOLIDATION A
TRANSWORLD NEWS

A

See note on consolidation pages on TB page xii.

Exercise A Business News

Answers: Differences: *Rail fares will rise/rail fares have risen; by 2 per cent/10 per cent; National Trailers will raise their prices/have raised their prices; one container ship/two container ships; the other banks are considering whether to charge/have decided not to charge; SS Titainia sank and Arctic Queen picked up crew/Arctic Queen sank and SS Titainia picked up crew; £1m/£2m compensation*

The information about the British post code system is for those SS who are interested. If you want to follow it up, ask which major English cities these post codes refer to:

L42 6RD	(Liverpool)
NE3 2PA	(Newcastle-on-Tyne)
SW1 3DD	(London, Southwest district)
M21 4JP	(Manchester)
CM2 9BE	(Cambridge)
PR2 4LN	(Preston)
RG21 3XS	(Reading)
BN6 7DL	(Brighton)
DH1 6FT	(Durham)
DL13 2UR	(Darlington)

Clock article
The roman numeral for four is usually written IIII on clocks but IV elsewhere.

Typing error article
Our *freight forwarding business* is expanding and we need *an AIRFREIGHT CLERK*. If you have *experience* in this *type* of work, contact Graham Davis, *Assistant Manager*...

WORKBOOK ANSWERS

Test A *1–c 2–a 3–b 4–d 5–a 6–b 7–c 8–d 9–a 10–c 11–b 12–d 13–b 14–b 15–d*

UNIT SIX
DISTRIBUTION
6

Language:	Reported questions The passive Countries
Business/Commerce:	Telephone messages and enquiries Standard business letter phrases: *I would be grateful if you could...* The work of a freight forwarder (*cont*) The distribution of manufactured goods Oral (and written) presentation Telexing flight information

TEACHING NOTES

Exercise 6.1 Listening comprehension

Answers: *1 Mr White from Colourco 2 Miss Green from Tanners 3 Mr Black from Rainbow Co Ltd 4 Ms Brown from Prism & Co 5 Mrs Scarlet from Dyers 6 Mr Grey from Spectrum*

Aim: Listening comprehension.

Ask SS check questions about the situation on SB page 46. Read through the list of people and companies with them before you play the tape (you could take this opportunity to revise the pronunciation of company names and use of titles). Play the tape as many times as necessary for the SS to work out who left which message and which company they were from. Most of the information is given directly on the tape, but SS will have to deduce that *Mr White* is the only man not accounted for in the first message (Sandra says '... wanting to know whether *he* can send ...'), that *Prism & Co* is the only company left for message 4 and that Mrs Scarlet is the only remaining *she* in message 5.

Exercise 6.2 Reported questions (LD)

Answers: *See LDT*

Aim: Presentation of reported questions.

Remind SS of the basic tense changes for reported speech. One way of presenting the word order changes for reported questions is to replay the tape for Exercise 6.1 for SS to take down as a dictation. Alternatively, you could ask SS to look at the language notes for this unit and work out the answers and 'rules' for themselves. The tape could then be used for them to check their own answers.

NB An alternative form to 'He asked *whether* Anne was going.' is 'He asked *if* Anne was going.'

For further practice of reported questions see WB Exercise 13a.

Exercise 6.3 Flight information (LD A & B)

Answers: *See LDT for suggestions on times.*

Aim: Practice of times on the 12- and 24-hour clocks in context.

Revise with SS how to say times on the 12- and 24-hour clocks (SS can revise from the language notes for this unit before the lesson if preferred). Set up the dialogue (see notes on TB pages xvii–xix) for SS to do in open or closed pairs.
WB Exercise 6b gives further practice of times.

If necessary, do additional work on times, eg you say a time on either the 12- or 24-hour clock and SS convert it. Alternatively SS can suggest times to one another to be converted. This can be done as a team game.

Exercise 6.4 Dictation

Answers: *2 Is there a flight from Hamburg to Manchester? 3 How long does the flight to Cairo take? 4 Is there a flight to Geneva on Sundays? 5 What time does the Brussels flight arrive? 6 When does the Paris flight leave? 7 Is there a morning flight to London?*

Aim: Listening practice and practice of direct and reported questions.

The questions are in reported form on the tape and SS have to write the direct form. The ideal would be for them to listen, transform the questions from indirect to direct in their heads and write down the direct questions. If this is not possible, however, SS can either write down the questions in indirect form and then transform them, or they can write down notes (eg *flight from Hamburg–Manchester*) which they then reconstitute as direct questions. As the questions are repeated on the tape, you should only need to play it once through.

A possible additional activity is to ask SS to write out some of the questions in the form of telephone messages.

Exercise 6.5 Telephone enquiries (LD)

Answers: *See LDT*

Aim: Further practice of reported questions in an authentic telephone dialogue; revision of country names.

Before SS do this exercise, they might like to revise country names in WB Exercise 6d. Elicit from SS the names of the countries where Transworld have branches. Present the dialogue (see notes on TB page xix) and then ask SS to practise it in closed pairs, referring to the Transworld brochure, but not to the dialogue.

The company abbreviations *GmbH*, *SARL* etc are the local equivalents of *plc* or *Ltd* to show that they are limited

companies (see Unit 10). Note that the company laws in each country are slightly different so there is no direct equivalent to each one.
NB *Enquiry* and *inquiry* are almost exactly the same. In British English *enquiry* is usually used about a request for information (*Thank you for your enquiry about our products*) and *inquiry* about a long and serious study (*an inquiry into the cure for a disease*).

Exercise 6.6 Reported questions (LD A & B)

Answers: *See LDT*

Aim: Question practice and further practice of reported questions.

This exercise can be done in 'open' groups of three round the class (see notes on open pairs on TB pages xvii–xix). The reported questions (in the form in LD B) can be written for homework. Make sure SS know that there is no question mark in reported questions).

Exercise 6.7 Telephone conversations

Aim: Fluency practice; consolidation of telephone enquiries.

Ask SS to work in pairs and prepare the six conversations, then pick on six different pairs to 'perform' their telephone conversations to the class (without a script). SS should consolidate their work on question forms and telephone enquiries from Exercise 6.5. You can afford to be quite strict in correcting SS' mistakes in this exercise – or in a sympathetic class, asking other SS to suggest corrections. SS can be asked to write out one of the telephone conversations in class or for homework.

Exercise 6.8 Distribution of manufactured goods

Answers: *1–c 2–a 3–h 4–f 5–d 6–g 7–b 8–e*

Aim: Reading comprehension; presentation of commercial information/vocabulary.

SS should be able to deduce the answers to this exercise from the reading passage and diagram. When they have done the exercise, though, you can ask further check questions about the passage and the diagram (or SS ask one another questions). The vocabulary in this exercise should be revised/tested regularly.
NB Selling goods *in bulk* is also called selling goods *wholesale*.

Exercise 6.9 The passive (LD)

Answers: *See LDT*

Aim: Revision of the passive.

If SS are not confident about the use of the passive, they can do this exercise while referring to the language notes for the unit. It can be done in class or for homework.
WB Exercise 6a gives further practice with passive sentences.

Exercise 6.10 Word puzzle

Answer: *1 raw materials* *2 wholesaler* *3 in bulk* *4 supply* *5 factory* *6 retailer* *7 produce* *8 domestic market* *9 warehouse* *10 exporter* *11 components* *12 freight forwarder* Hidden word: *manufacturer*

Aim: Vocabulary consolidation.

SS can work out the answers to this puzzle by referring to the text in Exercise 6.8. It can be done in class or for homework.

Exercise 6.11 Oral (and written) presentation

See TB pages xxi–xxii.

Exercise 6.12 Requesting information in a letter

Answers: *1 I would be grateful if you could tell me what your freight rates are.* *2 I would be grateful if you could tell me how much it costs to send a small package airfreight.* *3 I would be grateful if you could tell me what sort of packing is necessary for typewriters.* *4 I would be grateful if you could tell me where the nearest airport to Cannes is.* *5 I would be grateful if you could tell me what time the ship will arrive in Manchester.* *6 I would be grateful if you could tell me how big standard containers are.* *7 I would be grateful if you could tell me how long it takes to send goods by air to Greece.* *8 I would be grateful if you could tell me what time the morning flight leaves for Tokyo.*

Aim: Further practice of reported questions in a form suitable for business letters.

SS will probably already know the form *I would be grateful if you could*... (note that you cannot substitute *whether* for *if* in this phrase) and the rules of reported questions, so this exercise can be given for homework. Note that there are no tense changes because the 'asking verb' is in the present.

Oral preparation in class, if required, could be in the form *He wants to know what your freight rates are.* To make this more realistic, you could ask other SS to suggest answers or make responses such as *I'm afraid I don't know. I'll find out for you.*

Exercise 6.13 Telexing flight information

Answers: Sample telexes: *See page 51.*

Aim: Comprehension and production of telexes.

SS have already looked at the format of telexes in Unit 4 and should understand the few abbreviations used in these (for further work on abbreviations see Unit 11 and WB Exercise 6c). Ask questions before SS do this exercise to check their comprehension, then prepare the first telex with the class on the board, taking suggestions from the SS and then refining the final version. Ask them to do the remaining two telexes working in pairs. Since they are given models for both questions and answers, they should be able to work out acceptable answers.

```
GLM ENGING 22819 G
TRANSWLD 668013 G MANCHESTER 11/04   1605
ATTN STORKE
DAILY DEPARTURE BA962 MANCHESTER FRANKFURT VIA BIRMINGHAM 0800+

REGARDS
LONG
TRANSWLD 668013 G
GLM ENGING 22819 G
```

```
TRANSWLD 668013 G
BOS 81259 G  MANCHESTER 11/04  1400
ATTN LONG
PLS INFORM ARRIVAL TIME AND FREQUENCY TP/BA 458 LISBON MANCHESTER+ ?

REGARDS
BAKER
BOS 81259 G
TRANSWLD 668013 G
```

```
CYPRUS IMP 5138CY
TRANSWLD 668013 G  MANCHESTER  12/04  0930
ATTN PASSAS
BOS ORDER 06325 ARRIVING FLIGHT CY/BA358 1330 WED 13 +
REGARDS
LONG
TRANSWLD 668013 G
CYRPUS IMP 5138 CY
```

LABORATORY DRILLS TAPESCRIPT

Drill 6.2

Report the questions people asked about your company, like this:

P(M): Can I send a container to Turin?
R: *He asked whether he could send a container to Turin.*

Now you try.

P(F): Do you carry live animals?
R: *She asked whether we carried live animals.*
P(M): Is it cheaper to send goods by road or rail?
R: *He asked whether it was cheaper to send goods by road or rail.*
P(F): Can you collect goods from our factory?
R: *She asked whether we could collect goods from their factory.*
P(F): Do you handle containers?
R: *She asked whether we handled containers.*
P(M): What are your European trailer charges?
R: *He asked what our European trailer charges were.*

Aim: Practice of reported question forms
NB Note the changes to the pronouns.

Drill 6.3A

Say these times from the 24-hour clock as we usually say them, like this:

P: Oh eight hundred
R: *That's eight o'clock in the morning.*

Now you try.

P: Eleven thirty-five
R: *That's twenty-five to twelve in the morning.*
P: Thirteen forty-five
R: *That's quarter to two in the afternoon.*
P: Fifteen hundred
R: *That's three o'clock in the afternoon.*
P: Eighteen twenty-five
R: *That's twenty-five past six in the evening.*
P: Twenty-two oh five
R: *That's five past ten at night.*

Aim: Practice of times on the 12-hour and 24-hour clock

Drill 6.3B

Say these times from the 12-hour clock as we say them on the 24-hour clock, like this:

P: Eight o'clock in the morning
R: *That's oh eight hundred on the 24-hour clock.*

Now you try.

P: Half-past ten in the morning
R: *That's ten thirty on the 24-hour clock.*
P: Two o'clock in the afternoon
R: *That's fourteen hundred on the 24-hour clock.*
P: Ten to three in the afternoon
R: *That's fourteen fifty on the 24-hour clock.*
P: Seven o'clock in the evening
R: *That's nineteen hundred on the 24-hour clock.*
P: Twenty past six in the morning
R: *That's six twenty on the 24-hour clock.*

Aim: Further practice of times on the 12-hour and 24-hour clock

Drill 6.5

Ask for information about the Transworld branches, like this:

P: Australia
R: *Could you tell me whether you've got a branch in Australia?*
P: Yes. There's one in Sydney.
R: *How can I get in touch with your Sydney office?*

Now you try.

P: Germany
R: *Could you tell me whether you've got a branch in Germany?*

P: Yes. There's one in Hamburg.
R: *How can I get in touch with your Hamburg office?*
P: Sweden
R: *Could you tell me whether you've got a branch in Sweden?*
P: Yes. There's one in Stockholm.
R: *How can I get in touch with your Stockholm office?*
P: Italy
R: *Could you tell me whether you've got a branch in Italy?*
P: Yes. There's one in Milan.
R: *How can I get in touch with your Milan office?*

Aim: Practice of direct and indirect questions in context

Drill 6.6A

Ask questions about Transworld, like this:

P: Ask them whether they arrange transportation.
R: *Do you arrange transportation?*

Now you try.

P: Ask them whether they prepare documentation.
R: *Do you prepare documentation?*
P: Ask them whether they handle containers.
R: *Do you handle containers?*
P: Ask them whether they handle imports.
R: *Do you handle imports?*
P: Ask them whether they can advise us on the best means of transport.
R: *Can you advise us on the best means of transport?*
P: Ask them whether they can do our packing.
R: *Can you do our packing?*
P: Ask them whether they can advise us on our quotations to customers.
R: *Can you advise us on our quotations to customers?*

Aim: Recognition of indirect questions and practice of direct questions

Drill 6.6B

Report the questions you are asked about Transworld, like this:

P(M): Do you arrange transportation?
R: *He wanted to know whether we arranged transportation.*

Now you try.

P(F): Do you prepare documentation?
R: *She wanted to know whether we prepared documentation.*
P(M): Do you handle containers?
R: *He wanted to know whether we handled containers.*
P(F): Do you handle imports?
R: *She wanted to know whether we handled imports.*
P(F): Can you advise us on the best means of transport?
R: *She wanted to know whether we could advise them on the best means of transport.*
P(M): Can you do our packing?
R: *He wanted to know whether we could do their packing.*

P: Can you advise us on our quotations to customers?
R: *He wanted to know whether we could advise them on their quotations to customers.*

Aim: Practice of reported questions in the past

Drill 6.9

Talk in the passive about the distribution of manufactured goods, like this:

P: They produce finished goods from raw materials.
R: *Finished goods are produced from raw materials.*

Now you try.

P: The places where they produce goods are called factories.
R: *The places where goods are produced are called factories.*
P: They sell goods on the domestic market.
R: *Goods are sold on the domestic market.*
P: They usually sell goods to a wholesaler.
R: *Goods are usually sold to a wholesaler.*
P: Then they supply the goods to retailers.
R: *Then the goods are supplied to retailers.*
P: They sell the goods to individual customers.
R: *The goods are sold to individual customers.*
P: People usually store goods in warehouses.
R: *Goods are usually stored in warehouses.*

Aim: Practice of the passive form

WORKBOOK ANSWERS

Exercise 6a Passive and active sentences

3 Sandra 4 Kevin 5 Liz 6 Mr Storke 7 We don't know. 8 Mr Milgrom

Exercise 6b Times

2 2117 3 1000 4 1830 5 2300 6 0640 7 1605 8 0001

Exercise 6c Telex abbreviations

2 +? 3 PLS 4 ATTN 5 WED 6 THU

Exercise 6d Countries

Australia, Brazil, France, Germany, Italy, Japan, (the) Netherlands, Norway, Singapore, Spain (Spain is not mentioned in the SB), Sweden, (the) USA

1 = S	*2 = E*	*3 = G*	*4 = P*	*5 = N*	*6 = H*
7 = L	*8 = D*	*9 = C*	*10 = W*	*11 = A*	*12 = T*
13 = Z	*14 = U*	*15 = O*	*16 = M*	*17 = I*	*18 = J*
19 = R	*20 = Y*	*21 = B*	*22 = F*		

UNIT SEVEN
FOREIGN EXCHANGE

7

Language:	First conditional *Start doing* Present perfect progressive tense
Business/Commerce:	A view of the economy International trade figures Visible/invisible imports/exports Balance of Trade and Payments Currency exchange Oral presentation A letter of enquiry to a holiday advertisement

TEACHING NOTES

Exercise 7.1 Listening comprehension

Answers: *1 In the bin* *2 Europe* (In Britain, Europe is frequently referred to as 'the Continent'. NB We say *in* Europe, but *on* the Continent.) *3 Less* *4 Fewer* *5 Up* *6 (a)*

Aim: Listening comprehension and deduction of the meaning of words from context.

Pre-teach the words *economy* (the financial situation of a country) and *currency* (the type of money used by a country). Then play the tape as many times as necessary for SS to work out the correct answers to the exercise.

Use the exercise as the starting point for a short discussion about your country's economy (or the economy of the country the SS are now in) and the way it affects the lives of the SS. (It affects the price of goods in the shops, the foreign goods they can buy, the number of tourists and business people visiting the country, the number of your SS going on holiday abroad, the number of your country's goods sold abroad etc).

You could also use the exercise to highlight the difference between *fewer* (with a count noun) and *less* (with a mass noun) – a distinction which is now becoming blurred for many native speakers, including the BBC, but not for examiners! Since there are several comparatives in the next exercise, you could revise these forms in preparation for it.

Exercise 7.2 An economic model

Answers: *b prices abroad cheaper for Spaniards* *c fewer foreigners buy Spanish goods* *d fewer foreigners visit Spain* *e more Spaniards travel abroad* *f Spanish economy gets worse*

Aim: Revision of comparatives; focus on note-taking.

SS can use the notes in the completed part of the diagram to write their opposites in the other half. If you wish to focus particularly on the sorts of words which are omitted from notes (and telexes, newspaper headlines etc), see Exercise 11.10.

When checking the SS' answers, ask them to practise ways of expressing cause and effect, eg The peseta is strong, *so/therefore* Spanish prices are more expensive for foreigners. The peseta is strong. *This means that* Spanish prices etc. Spanish prices are more expensive for foreigners *because* the peseta is strong.

Exercise 7.3 First conditional (LD A & B)

Answers: *See LDT for sample answers.*

Aim: Presentation of the first conditional.

If you practised expressions of cause and effect in the previous exercise, then the concept of the first conditional will be clear. It is therefore just a case of presenting the form (see language notes for this unit). The division of the first conditional into two parts is much more common in spoken English than using a 'complete' conditional sentence.
Do the exercise in open pairs.

Additional optional practice arising from this exercise is of country names and adjectives. Nominate one S to start in each case and then two others must complete the following sentence appropriately: S1 I went to *Poland*... S2 and met a *Pole*... S3 and bought a *Polish* car. It can be done as a team game.

Exercise 7.4 A view of the economy

Answer: *If the peseta is strong, Spanish prices will be more expensive for foreigners and prices abroad will be cheaper for Spaniards. This means that more Spaniards will travel abroad and fewer foreigners will visit Spain. It also means that fewer foreigners will buy Spanish goods, so the Spanish economy will get worse and the peseta will be weak.*

Aim: Practice of connected paragraph writing.

This exercise is the written consolidation of Exercises 7.2 and 7.3. It can be set for homework.

Exercise 7.5 International trade figures (LD) and Exercise 7.6 Present perfect progressive (LD A & B)

Answers: *See LDT* (Take other answers from the table.)

Aim: Revision of indirect questions, *start -ing* and the use of the past simple with *ago*; practice in saying large sums of money.

Before you do these exercises, revise how we say large sums of money and how we say years (eg 1965 – *nineteen sixty-five*). You could do this as a number dictation.

Quickly revise also the form start/stop + *ing* by asking SS to suggest sentences about themselves using these forms in the past tense with *ago* (eg *I started wearing glasses five years ago*.) If you write the SS' examples on the board, you can also use them to present the present perfect progressive used with *for* and *since* which is practised in Exercise 7.6. Both exercises can be done T–S, and then in open and closed pairs.
WB Exercise 7c gives further practice of perfect tenses.

Exercise 7.7 Visible and invisible imports and exports

Answers: *1 A visible export 2 A visible import 3 A visible export 4 An invisible export 5 An invisible import 6 An invisible import 7 An invisible export 8 A visible export*

Aim: Presentation of commercial vocabulary/information.

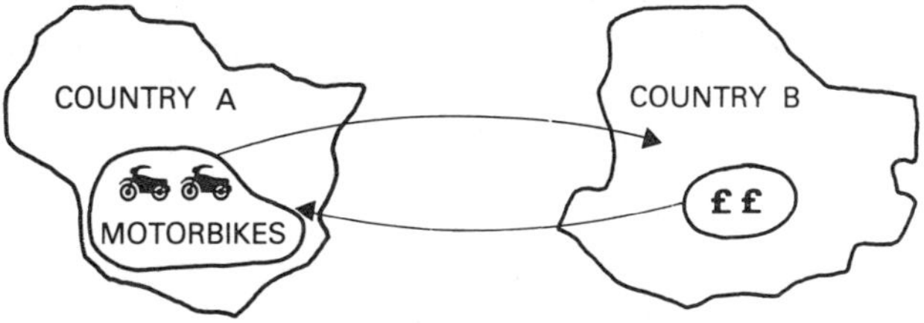

This is a visible export for A and a visible import for B.

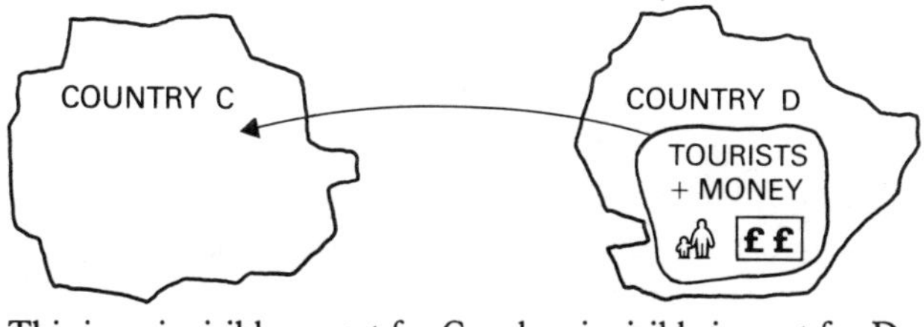

This is an invisible export for C and an invisible import for D.

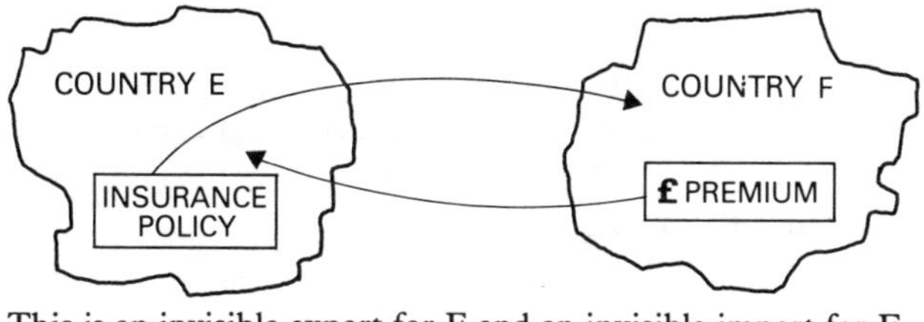

This is an invisible export for E and an invisible import for F.

The information in this text is best presented by the T with the help of diagrams like the ones on page 57 showing the passage of money from one country to another (the important thing is to remember where the money goes: a country which pays money is importing and a country which receives money is exporting).

SS can do the exercise in pairs or for homework, using the text for reference if necessary. You should pre-teach *expert* (someone who has a very good knowledge of his/her job) and *service* (work done for someone).

Exercise 7.8 Balance of Trade and Balance of Payments

Answers: *(a) −425* *(b) +400* *(c) nothing* *(d) −400* *(e) nothing* *(f) −25* *(g) +550* *(h) −200* *(i) −50* *(j) +150* *(k) −600* *(l) +1,200* *(m) −300* *(n) nothing* (See tapescript in SB for details)

Aim: Consolidation of commercial knowledge; listening practice.

If SS can work out the missing figures, it will mean that they have understood the two tables. The tape (or tapescript) explains how to complete the table in this exercise if they are still having difficulties. NB All figures in the imports column should be minus (−) and all the figures in the exports column plus (+).

Exercise 7.9 Favourable and unfavourable balances

Answers: *S: Trade–deficit; Payments–deficit* *X: Trade–deficit; Payments–surplus;* *Y: Trade–deficit; Payments–deficit* *W: Trade–surplus; Payments–surplus*

Aim: Presentation of commercial knowledge/vocabulary.

SS should be able to do this exercise (in open pairs) from the available information whether or not they completed the table in the previous exercise.

Exercise 7.10 A letter of enquiry

Answers: *A student staying in a foreign hotel is an invisible import for the student's country:*

Sample letter: *See page 59.*

Aim: Letter writing practice.

SS know enough language to be able to write this letter without help – possibly for homework.
NB These language/learning holidays are genuine and the proprietors of Fairfield House (John and Susan Norman) welcome *genuine* enquiries.

Exercise 7.11 Currency exchange

Answers: *(a) 1979* *(b) 30p* *(c) inflation* *(d) Dollardy* *(e) 1979* *(f) 60¢* *(g) the exchange rate* *(h) pound*

Student's address

Current date

The Manager
Fairfield House
High Street
Stanhope
Co Durham DL13 2UR
UK

Dear Sir or Madam

I saw your advertisement for activity holidays in the International Sun of 13 April. I would like to come for a holiday with my sister from 10 to 25 August.

I would be grateful if you could send me more information about the activities (do you have a fixed programme?) and the price for full board (my sister and I would like to share a room). Does the price include the cost of the activities? Could you also tell me the best way to get there from London?

I look forward to hearing from you.

Yours faithfully

Signature.

Student's name

(i) $2.50 *(j) Dollardy* *(k) 16p* *(l) less*
(m) pound *(n) 40p* *(o) 10p* *(p) weak*

Aim: Reading comprehension involving commercial knowledge.

SS should be able to do this exercise without any preparation. It would also be challenging and worthwhile to ask a group of good SS to write a similar article from the point of view of Dollardy, comparing different items with a graph showing the Dollardy home prices. This should be done in conjunction with Exercise 7.12.

Exercise 7.12 Oral presentation

See note on TB pages xxi–xxii. You are not advised to do written follow-up to this exercise as it would be more profitable to write an article as suggested in Exercise 7.11.

LABORATORY DRILLS TAPESCRIPT

Drill 7.3A

Answer these questions from your completed economic model, like this:

P: What will happen if prices abroad are more expensive for Spaniards?
R: *Fewer Spaniards will travel abroad.*

Now you try.

P: What will happen if more foreigners buy Spanish goods?
R: *The Spanish economy will get better.*
P: What will happen if the Spanish economy gets better?
R: *The peseta will be strong.*
P: What will happen if Spanish prices are more expensive for foreigners?
R: *Fewer foreigners will visit Spain.*

P: What will happen if fewer foreigners visit Spain?
R: *The Spanish economy will get worse.*
P: What will happen if the Spanish economy gets worse?
R: *The peseta will be weak.*

Aim: Recognition of the first conditional in relation to economics and practice of the *will* form for prediction

Drill 7.3B

Answer these questions from your completed economic model, like this:

P: Will fewer foreigners visit Spain?
R: *Yes, if prices abroad are more expensive for Spaniards.*

Now you try.

P: Will more foreigners buy Spanish goods?
R: *Yes, if Spanish prices are cheaper for foreigners.*
P: Will the peseta be strong?
R: *Yes, if the Spanish economy gets better.*
P: Will Spanish prices be more expensive for foreigners?
R: *Yes, if the peseta is strong.*

P: Will fewer foreigners visit Spain?
R: *Yes, if Spanish prices are more expensive for foreigners.*
P: Will more Spaniards travel abroad?
R: *Yes, if prices abroad are less expensive for Spaniards.*

Aim: Practice of the form of the first conditional in relation to economics

Drill 7.5

Ask for further information about these statements, like this:

P: We sell computers.
R: *Could you tell us when you started selling computers?*

Now you try.

P: We export meat.
R: *Could you tell us when you started exporting meat?*
P: Tourists come to Y.
R: *Could you tell us when tourists started coming to Y?*
P: We sell insurance.
R: *Could you tell us when you started selling insurance?*

P: We import oil.
R: *Could you tell us when you started importing oil?*
P: We buy computers.
R: *Could you tell us when you started buying computers?*

Aim: Practice of *start* + verb-*ing* in polite requests for information

Exercise 7.6A Ask for further information about these statements, like this:

P: We sell computers.
R: *How long have you been selling them?*

Now you try.

P: We export meat.
R: *How long have you been exporting it?*
P: Tourists go to Y.
R: *How long have they been going there?*
P: We sell insurance.
R: *How long have you been selling it?*
P: We import oil?
R: *How long have you been importing it?*
P: We buy computers.
R: *How long have you been buying them?*

Aim: Practice of the form of the present perfect progressive tense and pronouns

Drill 7.6B Rephrase these statements, like this:

P: You started selling to S in 1980.
R: *Yes. We've been selling to S since 1980.*
P: You started selling to S three years ago.
R: *Yes. We've been selling to S for three years.*

Now you try.

P: You started exporting to X in 1975.
R: *Yes. We've been exporting to X since 1975.*
P: You started importing from W six years ago.
R: *Yes. We've been importing from W for six years.*
P: You started buying from V five years ago.
R: *Yes. We've been buying from V for five years.*
P: You started importing from W in 1977.
R: *Yes. We've been importing from W since 1977.*
P: Tourists started coming to X four years ago.
R: *Yes. Tourists have been coming to X for four years.*

Aim: Practice of the form of the present perfect progressive with *for* and *since*

WORKBOOK ANSWERS

Exercise 7a Opposites

3 dishonest 4 impossible 5 unfortunate 6 unemployed 7 irregular 8 uncomfortable 9 unload 10 disadvantage 11 ungrateful 12 inexpensive 13 unusual 14 impolite

15 unhelpful *16 inexperienced* *17 unfriendly* *18 infrequent*

Exercise 7b Time expressions

2 They sold me the goods two years ago. *3 They have been selling computers for two years.* *4 They have owned their property since 1980.* *5 They bought the office in 1971.* *6 The meeting is on Monday.* 7 This sentence does not need a preposition. (It is possible to say *He will deliver the goods by next week.*) *8 He arrived at ten o'clock exactly.*

Exercise 7c Perfect tenses

2 They've been handling containers for ten years. *3 How long have you known about that?* *4 Prices have been rising steadily since 1978.* *5 I've stayed/been staying in a hotel until now.* *6 I've been working/I've worked for Transworld for three years.* *7 She's been typing all morning.* *8 Transworld have owned that office for a long time.*

Exercise 7d Silent letters

1 consiGnment *2 wHich* *3 Wholesale* *4 stationEry* *5 receiPt* *6 Write* *7 foreiGner* *8 freiGHt* *9 Knife* *10 Know* *11 Honest*

UNIT EIGHT
BORROWING MONEY

8

Language:	Comparatives: *not as cheap*
	Mathematical calculations
	Question practice
	Word stress
	Use of the articles
	The former/the latter
	Punctuation and capital letters
Business/Commerce:	Loans and overdrafts
	The vocabulary of borrowing money
	Credit cards/travel and entertainment cards
	Note-taking
	Oral (and written) presentation
	A bank statement
	Business letter conventions

TEACHING NOTES

Exercise 8.1 Listening comprehension

Answers: *1 red* *2 account* *3 statement* *4 charges* *5 pay* *6 more* *7 overdrawn* *8 black* (NB SS must deduce this answer as it is not on the tape.)

Aim: Listening practice; deduction of vocabulary from context; presentation of commercial information.

Set the scene for this unit by discussing with SS their own experience of banks and borrowing money. Do not pre-teach the answers which the SS should be able to deduce. NB Although technically an account is overdrawn, we frequently use the expression *I'm overdrawn* to express this.

Exercise 8.2 Comparatives (LD)

Answers: *See LDT*

Aim: Presentation of the negative comparison *not as . . . (as)*.

SS have revised standard comparative forms in Unit 7. From the given model, SS should be able to do this exercise in open pairs. For homework the complete written form for each sentence can be prepared: *A loan is not as cheap as an overdraft.* WB Exercise 8b gives further practice of comparatives.

Exercise 8.3 Calculations (LD)

Sample answers (any of the forms in the language notes may be used): *a Six divided by two equals three.* *b Eight plus nine is seventeen.* *c Thirty minus six equals twenty-four.* *d Twenty divided by two is ten.* *e Seven times three is twenty-one.* *f Twelve plus five makes seventeen.* *g Twenty-three take away two is twenty-one.* *h Ninety-nine divided by nine makes eleven.* *i Twenty times four equals eighty.* *j Forty added to eleven makes fifty-one.* (NB The LD is different from the exercise.)

Aim: Practice of numbers and calculations.

SS will probably already know some of the ways of expressing calculations. You can either present the other possibilities, or refer SS to the language notes.
WB Exercise 8d gives further practice of calculations.

If SS need further practice of calculations (or if they need a lighter class activity) you could play the game BINGO with them. Prepare a card for each S which has twelve different numbers under 50 on it (or ask SS to write any twelve numbers under 50 on a card and give it to another S so that everyone has a card). The caller then calls out numbers at random (or draws them from a hat) and any S with that number on his/her card crosses it off. The first S to cross of all twelve numbers calls out *BINGO* and is the winner. The alternative version of this game is that the caller calls out a calculation to represent the number (eg the caller says *ten plus two* and any S with the number twelve crosses it off). It is advisable to ask different SS to call out the correct answer to the calculations as you go along to avoid problems or disappointments later.
NB The pronunciation of *minus* is /ˈmaɪnəs/.

Exercise 8.4 Borrowing money

Sample questions and answers: *How much was Anne's loan? (£600)* *Who lent Anne the money? (The bank)* *Who had a debt? (Anne)* *How much did Anne owe the bank? (£600 at the beginning)* *Who was the debtor? (Anne)* *Who was Anne's creditor? (The bank)* *How much did Anne repay in the first month? (£55 – £50 capital and £5 interest)* *How much did Anne repay in the second month? (£54.54 – £50 capital and £4.54 interest)* (Do not go into more detail than this as the calculations get increasingly difficult to work out without a calculator.)

Aim: Question practice; presentation of commercial knowledge and vocabulary.

Rather than doing this exercise as a reading comprehension, you can present the factual information with the help of diagrams on the blackboard and introduce the relevant vocabulary as appropriate. Alternatively you could ask a group of three or four SS who are good at maths to study the exercise for homework and let them present the information and vocabulary to the rest of the class in the next lesson.

The questions and answers are more to check comprehension of the vocabulary than comprehension of the concept. They can either be done in open pairs or as a team competition (points are awarded for correct questions – particularly in relation to correct use of new vocabulary – just as much as for correct answers).

WB Exercise 8a gives further practice of this vocabulary.

Exercise 8.5 Definitions (LD)

Answers: *See LDT*

Aim: Vocabulary consolidation; practice in defining words.

The exercise can be carried out as suggested in the SB, but it is profitable for SS to prepare their definitions in pairs first. You might limit each pair to preparing only three or four definitions to save time, but tell each S which words to prepare to avoid all the SS preparing the same words.

If you play the LD in class, SS can compare their definitions with those on the tape. Alternatively you can use the LD for revision in class in a later lesson.

Exercise 8.6 Word stress

Answers: *b BOR-row* *c re-PAY* *d DEBT-or* *e per CENT* *f per AN-num* *g IN-terest* (NB This word has only two syllables) *h BA-lance* *i CRE-di-tor* *j ac-COUNT* *k o-ver-DRAWN* *l in CRE-dit* *m O-ver-draft* *n trans-AC-tion* *o CAP-i-tal*

Aim: To focus the SS' attention on stress in words.

The rules about how exactly to divide words into syllables are very complicated and not worth spending time on, so as long as SS divide words into the correct number of syllables in approximately the right places, that is acceptable for this exercise. (NB For the same reason, encourage SS not to break words at the end of a line in written work.)

If SS already have some awareness of syllable-division and word stress, then do the exercise as directed in the SB. If they do not, or if the words are so unfamiliar still that they are uncertain, then play the tape one word at a time to allow SS to hear the syllable divisions and stress.

Note particularly the change in stress between *overDRAWN* and *Overdraft*. Note also that the main stress in an individual word can be lost if that word is combined in a phrase, eg *acCOUNT*, but *BANK account*.

For further practice of word stress see WB Exercise 12b.

Exercise 8.7 Articles

Answers: *1 The* *2 The* *3 the* *4 the* *5 a* *6 a* *7 the* *8 a* *9 the* *10 The* *11 the*

12 the	*13 a*	*14 the*	*15 a*	*16 The*	*17 the*
18 the	*19 the*	*20 a*	*21 the/a*	*22 the*	*23 the*
24 The	*25 a*	*26 the*	*27 the*	*28 the*	*29 the*
30 the					

Aim: Presentation of commercial information; consolidation of the use of articles.

Ask SS to do this exercise while referring to the language notes on the use of articles. It can be done for homework or in class (possibly in pairs). When you check through the answers, discuss with the SS the reason for each use of each article.

Ask SS to find out what VISA and MASTERCARD are called in your country.

Exercise 8.8 Note-taking

Answers: *A Yes* *B No* *C No* *D Yes* *E £17.50pa* *F Nothing* (except the interest you pay on money you do not repay at the end of the month) *G The full amount* *H £5 or 5 per cent of the bill* (whichever is greater) *I No* *J Yes* *K No* *L Yes* (on amounts he/she does not pay back each month) *M No* *N Yes*

Aim: Reading comprehension; assimilation of commercial information.

SS can do this exercise as a reading comprehension without preparation, although you can ask further comprehension questions afterwards if you feel it is necessary.

For your information, the following is the top copy of a sales voucher used with an Access card.

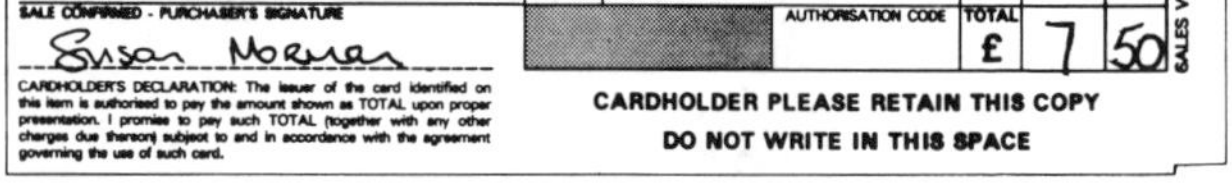
5224 0061 2345 6789

1265 01/82 12/83
MRS SUSAN NORMAN

7734313
R N SPORTS
NEWCASTLE UPON TYNE

SALE CONFIRMED - PURCHASER'S SIGNATURE
Susan Norman

CARDHOLDER'S DECLARATION: The issuer of the card identified on this item is authorised to pay the amount shown as TOTAL upon proper presentation. I promise to pay such TOTAL (together with any other charges due thereon) subject to and in accordance with the agreement governing the use of such card.

MasterCard

PLEASE WRITE FIRMLY WITH BALLPOINT PEN

DATE	SEND?	TAKE?	DEPT.	SALES No.	INITIALS
24·5·82		✓			SR

QUAN.	DESCRIPTION	Unit Cost	AMOUNT	
1	Squash Racket		7	50
	AUTHORISATION CODE	TOTAL £	7	50

CARDHOLDER PLEASE RETAIN THIS COPY
DO NOT WRITE IN THIS SPACE

CARDHOLDER'S COPY
SALES VOUCHER

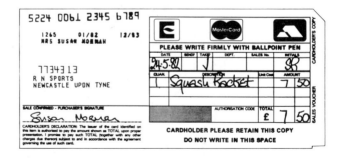

Exercise 8.9 The former/the latter

Answers: *1 The former were French and the latter were German.* *2 The former is for goods sent by air and the latter is for goods sent by sea.* *3 Access is an example of the latter.* *4 The former are free. You pay a subscription for the latter.* *5 The former is a request for goods, the latter (is) a request for payment.*

Aim: Presentation of the terms *former* and *latter*; revision of *order* and *invoice*.

SS should be able to do this exercise without preparation, so it could be set for homework. In the final example, SS have to use their knowledge of sales documentation.

Exercise 8.10 Oral (and written) presentation

See note on TB pages xxi–xxii. Asking the SS to talk about cheque cards is for revision of the information in Unit 2.

Exercise 8.11 A bank statement

Answers: Across: *a 20693056* *d 18* *e 53* *g 12* *h 45* *j 40* *k 1041* *m 261* *n 886282* Down: *a 28041983* *b 31* *c 08* *f 38152* *g 10* *i 50* *j 49228* *l 0104* *o 69*

Aim: Comprehension of a bank statement.

In order to do this puzzle, SS have to remember that dates below 10 can start with 0 (eg 08/04/1983 is 8th April 1983). SS should be able to do the puzzle without help, but afterwards you might want to ask further comprehension questions, eg *When was Anne overdrawn?* (28–29 March, 20 April) *How much was Anne's telephone bill?* (£35) *Which two words beginning 're-' mean payments into the account?* (remittance, receipt) *Why did the bank take off interest from Anne's account at the end of March?* (Because she had been overdrawn. NB SS will have to use their knowledge from earlier in the unit to answer this question.) *How much is Anne paid a year?* (Approximately £5907.36, which is £492.28 × 12 months. This is Anne's take-home pay after tax has been deducted.) etc.
WB Exercise 8c exploits the vocabulary in the bank statement.

Exercise 8.12 Punctuation

Answer: *See page 68.*

Aim: Punctuation practice and reading comprehension.

SS can refer to the language notes in this unit and the language notes to Unit 1 on business letter format and conventions.

Although it is better to teach SS one correct form for punctuation, the correct format of letters etc, certain points are slightly controversial or have acceptable alternatives:
The abbreviation *plc* can also be written *PLC* or *Plc*.
Some people prefer to write commas throughout an address, thus: *Ms A. Bell,*
69, Maple Road,
Manchester M3 2BY
Note that it is only correct to use a full stop after an abbreviation if the letters do not include the final letter of the

abbreviated word, eg Ltd (*Limited*) without a full stop, but Co. (*Co*mpany) because the word has been 'interrupted'. It is perfectly correct, however, and modern usage to leave out all full stops after abbreviations.

Some people like to have a comma after the opening and closing salutation. This has no effect on the first sentence of the body of the letter which should still start with a capital. Some people do not like the title 'Ms' which they associate with the feminist movement, but it does seem to be a sensible alternative to making a mistake with a woman's title. Many men do not write their title (or even their first name) under their signature, because they assume that everyone in business must be male unless otherwise stated. In international trade, where foreign first names may not be familiar to other nationalities, it is sensible for all letter writers to give their full name and title.

BONDS BANK plc
CITY BRANCH
25 High Street Manchester M1 2AA

Ms A Bell
69 Maple Road
Manchester M3 2BY

20 April 1983

Dear Ms Bell

I am sorry to inform you that your account is overdrawn by £18.10. I would not usually bother about such a small amount, but you regularly overdraw your account at the end of each month without informing us. I would be grateful if you would come in to talk to me about this as soon as possible.

Yours sincerely

T Gregory

Mr Terence Gregory
Manager

LABORATORY DRILLS TAPESCRIPT

Drill 8.2

Pretend to misunderstand these statements and then correct yourself, like this:

P: An overdraft is usually cheaper than a loan.
R: *So a loan is cheaper.*
P: No.
R: *So a loan isn't as cheap.*

Now you try.

P: That's right. The first invoice was higher than the second.
R: *So the second invoice was higher.*
P: No.
R: *So the second invoice wasn't as high.*
P: That's right. PDT's goods are more expensive than GLM's.
R: *So GLM's goods are more expensive.*
P: No.
R: *So GLM's goods aren't as expensive.*
P: That's right. BOS's delivery is quicker than PDT's.
R: *So PDT's delivery is quicker.*
P: No.
R: *So PDT's delivery isn't as quick.*
P: That's right. BOS's prices are lower than GTG's.
R: *So GTG's prices are lower.*
P: No.
R: *So GTG's prices aren't as low.*
P: That's right. Smith's cloth is better than Jones's.
R: *So Jones's cloth is better than Smith's.*
P: No.
R: *So Jones's cloth isn't as good.*
P: That's right.

Aim: Practice of positive and negative comparative forms

Drill 8.3

Give the answers to these calculations, like this:

P: Five multiplied by four
R: *Twenty*

Now you try.
(The example is not repeated)

P: Ten divided by two
R: *Five*
P: Twenty minus two
R: *Eighteen*
P: Ten plus five
R: *Fifteen*
P: Three times three
R: *Nine*
P: Forty-four divided by four
R: *Eleven*
P: A hundred minus two
R: *Ninety-eight*
P: Sixty plus twelve
R: *Seventy-two*
P: Eight multiplied by two
R: *Sixteen*
P: Fifteen divided by five
R: *Three*
P: Seventeen and three
R: *Twenty*

Aim: Practice of numbers and comprehension of calculations

NB This LD is different from the exercise.

Drill 8.5

Say which words in Exercise 8.5 are being defined, like this:

P: Your account is in the red. In other words, your account is . . .
R: *Overdrawn*

Now you try.
(The example is not repeated)

P: Someone you owe money to is your . . .
R: *Creditor*
P: Someone who owes money to you is your . . .
R: *Debtor*

P: This is the cost of borrowing money. When you borrow money from the bank, you pay the bank . . .
R: *Interest*
P: To pay back money. In other words, to . . .
R: *Repay*
P: If you have money in your account, your account is . . .
R: *In credit*
P: You have some money in the bank. In other words, you have a bank . . .
R: *Account*
P: You are repaying £3,000 every year. In other words, you are repaying £3,000 . . .
R: *Per annum*
P: You've taken more money out of your account than you had in it. In other words you have an . . .
R: *Overdraft*
P: The sum of money which you borrow and which you must repay is called . . .
R: *Capital*
P: The bank lends you money. This is money which you . . .
R: *Borrow*
P: This means part of a hundred. For example, your interest might be calculated at ten . . .
R: *Per cent*
P: You buy something. You take money out of the bank. Each of these events is a . . .
R: *Transaction*
P: The document the bank sends you showing all your transactions is called a . . .
R: *Statement*
P: When you've borrowed some money and paid back some of it, the money you still have to repay is called the . . .
R: *Balance*

Aim: Practice of new vocabulary

WORKBOOK ANSWERS

Exercise 8a A loan

2 Anne 3 Tom 4 Tom 5 Anne 6 20% pa 7 £100 8 £100.

Exercise 8b Comparisons

3 faster than 4 cheaper than 5 slower than 6 not as quick as 7 bigger than 8 not as small as

Exercise 8c Vocabulary puzzle

2 receipt 3 payment 4 overdrawn 5 DR 6 date 7 interest 8 statement 9 remittance 10 account 11 notes 12 balance forward 13 details

Exercise 8d Calculations

b 8 minus 5 equals/is 3 c 4 times 6 equals 24 d 20 divided by 4 is 5 e 9 plus 9 equals 18 f 18 divided by 9 equals 2 g 18 minus 9 is 9 h 2 times 2 equals 4/2 plus 2 equals 4

UNIT NINE
COMPUTERISED ACCOUNTS

9

Language:	The passive (*revision*) Alphabetical order Countries/nationalities Confirming question tags (*revision*) *Yes/no* questions *Going to do* *Was going to do*
Business/Commerce:	Writing a letter from dictation Parts of a computer Accounting procedures A 'computer program' Dealing with correspondence A telephone conversation Comparison of standard phrases in telexes, telephone conversations and formal business letters

TEACHING NOTES

Exercise 9.1 Corrections (LD)

Answers: *See LDT*

Aim: Listening comprehension; practice of the passive.

Treat the introductory picture sequence as a reading comprehension and ask questions to check SS' comprehension. Then play the tape for SS to do this exercise. They should already know the passive form.

Exercise 9.2 A letter

Answer: *See page 72.*

Aim: Dictation; practice of business letter format.

This exercise can be done as a dictation in class (playing the tape as often as necessary) and then written out with the correct format for homework.

Exercise 9.3 Computers (LD)

Sample answers: *See LDT*

Aim: Practice of *yes/no* questions; presentation of commercial information; reading comprehension.

Introduce this text by asking SS what they already know about computers – and introduce some of the relevant vocabulary. The text explains all the computer vocabulary so SS should not find it difficult.

(See Exercise 9.2)

Brighter Office Supplies
Limited

MANCHESTER BRANCH
17 Cedar Street
Manchester M2 6HD

Accounts Department
Transworld Freight plc
74 Dockside
Manchester M15 7BJ

6 May 1983

Our ref: GB/sn
Your ref: 003476

Dear Sirs

Thank you for your usual monthly statement. It says we have to pay you nothing. The one you sent last month said the same, so I now enclose our cheque for no pounds no pence. Will this perhaps be the last time you send a statement of this kind?

Yours faithfully

G. Best

Mr Geoffrey Best
Chief Accounts Clerk

Give them time to prepare questions about the text before they ask and answer them in open pairs. Remind SS to prepare at least one question of each type (a *yes* question, a *no* question and a question which the computer will not answer).

Alternatively, each S can prepare six questions for homework. These are then given to another S in class who writes the answers (and makes any necessary corrections to the questions). A third S can correct both questions and answers and/or the T can collect them for marking.
NB Computers can be programmed to accept questions other than yes/no questions, but the principle that at each stage of an operation it only has a choice of two responses is always true.

You might focus on the difference in meaning between *program* and *programme* (see Unit 4 language notes).
GIGO is pronounced /gi:gəʊ/

Exercise 9.4 Computer tape

Answers: *1 visual display unit* *2 program* *3 computer terminal* *4 output* *5 central processing unit* *6 GIGO* *7 data* *8 store* *9 find* *10 process*

Aim: Vocabulary consolidation.

This is another kind of word puzzle which SS can do in class or at home. All the words are to do with computers and can be found in the text in Exercise 9.3.

Exercise 9.5 A computer program (LD)

Answers: *1–E* *2–B (In that case, I'm still going to send a credit note.)* *3–A* *4–C* *5–F* *6–D* *7–G (I'm still going to send a receipt.) See also LDT*

Aim: Practice of *going to* future and *was going to*; to help SS understand the principles of a computer program; consolidation of sales documents.

While doing this exercise, one S in each pair should cover the problems and only look at the 'computer program'. The other S should only look at the problems. By working through the program, SS should consolidate their knowledge about some sales documents, but they should also learn what a *debit note* and *credit note* are. SS will probably already have met the *going to* future. If so, the form *was going to* will be a very straightforward extension and can be understood from the context. Since David's answers to 2 and 7 are correct, the concept is clear that *was going to* is used for a past intention. That intention may now have changed, or it may still be the same. *Pos* and *neg* stand for *positive* (yes) and *negative* (no).
NB See note on future forms on TB page 78.
WB Exercise 9c further consolidates sales documentation.

Exercise 9.6 The alphabet (LD A & B)

Answers: *See LDT. Also ABD, BLT, FPT, GLM, HEQ, JBX, JDR, JLN, VDU, WRS, ZYZ, ZZY.*

Aim: Practice of letters of the alphabet, country names and adjectives and question tags.

Listen to the LD for the correct intonation of the question tag and possibly use it as a model for the SS in class. SS can determine which country the companies are in from the abbreviation in the name (in each case it is the abbreviation for the equivalent of a private or public limited company in each country – see Unit 10 for the difference between types of business). To make the exercise more realistic, ask SS to study the Transworld brochure on SB page 49 to determine which abbreviation is used in each country (see TB note to Exercise 6.5). They should then do the exercise, trying to remember which abbreviation is used in which country. Note that the positive question tag used with a positive statement (in the LD) is used to express interest. It is not a genuine question.

Exercise 9.7 A telephone conversation

Answers: The order is: *5, 4, 8, 1, 9, 7, 11, 10, 3, 12, 6, 2*

Aim: Reading comprehension; revision of phone language.

When SS have put the dialogue in the right order, ask them to act it out in pairs and improvise other similar dialogues.

Exercise 9.8 Information transfer

Answers: *1 (letter) I'm afraid we haven't received your payment. REGRET REMITTANCE NOT RECEIVED 2 (telephone) We would be grateful if you could send us the order number at your earliest convenience. PLS SEND ORDER NO. SOONEST 3 (telex) I am sorry to inform you that consignment (reference 8934) was damaged. I'm afraid consignment 8934 was damaged. 4 (letter) Please send us the documents as soon as you can. PLS SEND DOCUMENTS SOONEST 5 (telex) We would be grateful if you could send the flight details at your earliest convenience. Please send us the flight details as soon as you can. 6 (telephone) I am sorry to inform you that the ship has not arrived yet. REGRET SHIP NOT ARRIVED*

Aim: Practice of standard business phrases focussing on the differences between alternative forms of communication.

SS can find the equivalent phrases in the three different forms of communication in the exercise itself to use as the model. You could use the exercise as the basis of a short discussion about the different forms of communication, why each is used and how the language in them differs.

Exercise 9.9 In-tray exercise

Sample answers: *1 I'm going to give it to Liz in the accounts department. 2 I'm going to retype the telephone list (number 4). 3 I'm going to give it to Graham Davis. I'm not going to open it because it's personal. 4 (See 2.) 5 I'm going to give it to Graham Davis. SS can see from the telephone list that Edward Payne – who the subscription is for – used to be the Branch Manager, but now that position is held by Graham Davis. Alternatively, SS might say 'I'm going to send it to Edward Payne (at his new address).' 6 I'm not going to do anything with it. (But see 12.) I'm going to file it. 7 I'm going to give the message to Graham Davis./I'm going to remind Graham Davis that he is going to London tomorrow. (See diary.) 8 I'm going to tell Liz in the accounts department. 9 I'm going to ring the photocopier company again about it – and then I'm going to tell Nick the answer. (See also 12.) 10 I'm going to type the memo./I'm going to tell Graham Davis that Kevin Hughes will be on holiday on 17th May. 11 I'm going to give it to Kevin Hughes (the export manager). 12 I'm going to ring them to ask about their prices (they might be better than Telford Towels in 6 and the photocopying company – see 9). 13 I'm going to give it to Liz in the accounts department.*

Aim: Reading comprehension, skimming practice.

This exercise is the sort of thing anyone in an office might have to do. Sandra has to work out who to give most of the correspondence to, she does not have to do much about it herself. A person in a more senior position would have to decide which he/she would deal with him/herself and which could be delegated.

The exercise is best done in pairs so that an additional part of the task is for SS to decide how best to share the work. Put a time limit of 15–20 minutes on the exercise, but the last few minutes can be 'stretched' if a lot of the class still haven't finished. You are trying to encourage SS to read quickly, though, and not to dwell on unfamiliar vocabulary.

As suggested in the SB, SS can compare their decisions in small groups (possibly with each member of a pair being in a different group so each S takes responsibility for his/her own decisions). A whole class discussion will make sure all the SS have considered all the possible courses of action.

As further exploitation of this material, ask SS to make up questions about the correspondence to ask one another.
NB The telephone list (item 4) refers to Sam Poole as the *manifest clerk*. Tell the SS that a ship's *manifest* is the list of cargo it has on board and ask them what they think a manifest clerk's job is (to check each manifest to see which of their client's goods are or should be on board and to check that the correct goods are loaded or unloaded).

Exercise 9.10 Roleplay

This exercise is best done immediately after 9.9 if possible, while SS are still thinking about the correspondence. Most of the encounters will be very similar, based on the introductory dialogue to this unit. To keep the SS lively, you could warn them that from time to time you will clap your hands. If you do this, the two SS in any group who are speaking in role at that time should swap roles – without any break in the conversation! (See notes on roleplay on TB page xxi.)

You could ask SS to write answers to any or all of the following: 5, 6, 9, 10, 12 and 13.

Exercise 9.11 Telephone extension list

Answers: *Anne Bell 101, Graham Davis 200, Nick Dawson 302, Robert Drillsma 301, Kevin Hughes 203, David Laing 201, Jane Long 300, Sandra Parr 101, Sam Poole 303, Liz Shepherd 400, David Thompson 401, Bill Thomson 304, Neil Warner 202*
(NB The tapescript for this exercise is not printed in the SB.)

Aim: Number dictation; consolidation of alphabetical order.

The names should be put in order according to surnames not first names. SS will have to take into account the handwritten changes on the telephone list. Let them put the names into alphabetical order before they listen to the tape, which then becomes an automatic check on their order as well as providing the telephone extension numbers.

SS might be interested in the short forms or affectionate forms of English first names which are frequently used by family or friends. The following are fairly common: Anne–Annie; Nicholas–Nick; Robert–Rob, Bob, Robby, Bobby; Kevin–Kev; David–Dave, Davie; Sandra–Sandie; Samuel–Sam; Elizabeth–Liz, Lizzie, Beth, Betty (Queen Elizabeth II is called Lillibet by her family); William–Will, Bill, Willy, Billy; Richard–Rich, Richie, Rick, Dick; Thomas–Tom; Susan–Sue, Susie; Michael–Mike, Mick; Penelope–Penny etc. Note that a *nickname* is a name used instead of the person's own name by close associates, usually reflecting something to do with the person's name or character, eg Anne Bell might be called 'Ding-dong' (the sound of a bell), Samuel Poole might be called 'Swimming' (swimming pool), someone might be called 'Happy' because they smile a lot – or because they never smile!

LABORATORY DRILLS TAPESCRIPT

Drill 9.1

Re-phrase these sentences in the passive, like this:

P: Sandra opened the letter.
R: *The letter was opened by Sandra.*

Now you try.

P: The computer printed the statement.
R: *The statement was printed by the computer.*
P: Someone at BOS wrote the letter.
R: *The letter was written by someone at BOS.*
P: David sent the statement.
R: *The statement was sent by David.*
P: Liz wrote the letter of apology.
R: *The letter of apology was written by Liz.*

Aim: Practice of the passive form with an agent

Drill 9.3

Give short answers to these questions about the text in Exercise 9.3, like the computer:

P: Does data mean information?
R: *Yes*
P: Where are the microchips?
R: *Input error*

Now you try.
(The examples are not repeated)

P: Can a computer store information?
R: *Yes*
P: What is the CPU?
R: *Input error*

P: Does the CPU look like a television?
R: *No*
P: Is a VDU a terminal?
R: *Yes*
P: What other terminals are there?
R: *Input error*
P: What is output?
R: *Input error*
P: Is the information you put into a computer called output?
R: *No*
P: What does G-I-G-O stand for?
R: *Input error*

Aim: Text comprehension and recognition of question types

Drill 9.5

Say what you intended to do about these accounts, as if you are David in Exercise 9.5, like this:

P: What about BOS's account?
R: *I was going to send a statement at the end of the month.*

Now you try.

P: What about GLM's account?
R: *I was going to send a credit note.*
P: What about JLN's account?
R: *I was going to send a debit note.*
P: What about HEQ's account?
R: *I was going to send a reminder.*
P: What about WRS's account?
R: *I wasn't going to do anything.*
P: What about ZYZ's account?
R: *I was going to send an invoice.*
P: What about BLT's account?
R: *I was going to send a receipt.*

Aim: Practice of the form *was going to*

Drill 9.6A

Say the letters in the company names in Exercise 9.6, like this:

P: 1
R: *J B X*

Now you try.

P: 2
R: *J D R*
P: 3
R: *W R S*
P: 4
R: *J L N*
P: 5
R: *F P T*
P: 6
R: *B L T*
P: 7
R: *A B D*
P: 8
R: *G L M*
P: 9
R: *V D U*
P: 10
R: *H E Q*
P: 11
R: *Z Z Y*
P: 12
R: *Z Y Z*

Aim: Revision of the pronunciation of letters of the alphabet

Drill 9.6B

Express interest in the location of these companies, like this:

P: JBX is Singaporean.
R: *JBX is in Singapore, is it?*

Now you try. Be careful of the pronunciation of the question tag.

P: JDR is American.
R: *JDR is in America, is it?*
P: WRS is Norwegian.
R: *WRS is in Norway, is it?*

P: JLN is German.
R: *JLN is in Germany, is it?*
P: FPT is Brazilian.
R: *FPT is in Brazil, is it?*
P: BLT is French.
R: *BLT is in France, is it?*
P: ABD is British.
R: *ABD is in Britain, is it?*
P: GLM is Swedish.
R: *GLM is in Sweden, is it?*
P: VDU is Italian.
R: *VDU is in Italy, is it?*
P: HEQ is Australian.
R: *HEQ is in Australia, is it?*
P: ZZY is Japanese.
R: *ZZY is in Japan, is it?*
P: ZYZ is Dutch.
R: *ZYZ is in Holland, is it?* or
ZYZ is in the Netherlands, is it?

Aim: Practice of countries' names

Future forms
Since the *going to* future is introduced in this unit, you might like to revise the three different future forms SS know and the difference in meaning.

WILL is used (a) for prediction (*I think Italy will win the cup.*), (b) for a decision made at that moment about the future. (*I'll just go and wash my hands before dinner.*), (c) for an offer of help (*Just a minute. I'll open the door for you.*), (d) for polite requests (*Will/Would/Could you type this letter please?*).

GOING TO expresses an intention (*I'm going to get up late tomorrow. He's going to be a teacher when he grows up.*) It is not usually used with the verbs *come* or *go* when the present progressive is used instead.

The PRESENT PROGRESSIVE is used about future plans. It implies that the plans are definite or that arrangements have already been made (*I'm meeting John this evening.*) It is usually used with a time expression (or a time is known or implied) to differentiate it from its present meaning.

Compare:
1 *I'm going to visit my mother tonight.* (She probably doesn't know I'm going.)
I'm visiting my mother tonight (and she's baked me a cake).
2 *'We've run out of bread.' 'I know. I'm getting some tomorrow.'*
'We've run out of bread.' 'Oh have we? I'll get some tomorrow.'

WORKBOOK ANSWERS

Exercise 9a To

3 I want to 4 nothing 5 There used to be 6 I look forward to 7 nothing 8 The bill came to £50 9 nothing 10 nothing

Exercise 9b Vocabulary groups

1 Bill of Lading, air waybill, consignment note 2 telex, memo, letter 3 invoice, order, statement 4 claim, premium, policy 5 cargo, consignment, freight 6 dimensions, weight, volume

Exercise 9c Sales documentation

0001 receipt 0002 invoice 0003 credit note 0004 statement 0005 reminder

Exercise 9d A letter

TRANSWORLD FREIGHT PLC

74 Dockside
Manchester M15 7BJ

Tel: 061 8537272
Telex: 668013

Cables/telegrams: TRANSWLD MANCHESTER

Accounts Department
Household Designs & Co Ltd
22 High Street
Manchester M1 2BL

13 April 1983

Our ref: LS/sp
Your ref: 0455/0004

Dear Sirs

I am sorry to inform you that your invoice (ref 045/0004) dated 6 April is incorrect.

I have spoken to the employee who bought the chairs on our behalf and she told me that she had agreed a 10% discount on the price with your salesman.

I would be grateful if you could issue a credit note for £66.00 and adjust our next statement accordingly.

Yours faithfully

E. Shepherd

Elizabeth Shepherd (Mrs)
Senior accounts clerk

UNIT TEN
TYPES OF BUSINESS

10

Language:	Percentages and fractions
	Must/can
	Unlikely possibilities (second conditional)
	Question practice
Business/Commerce:	Setting up a limited company
	Types of business
	Note-taking
	A Memorandum of Association
	Describing graphs
	A simulation: Speculating

TEACHING NOTES

Exercise 10.1 Listening comprehension

Answers: *1–b 2–a 3–b 4–b 5–a 6–a 7–a 8–b 9–b 10–b*

Aim: Listening comprehension; presentation of commercial information.

Although the second conditional has not yet been formally presented to the SS, it is used in this dialogue to boost their confidence in being able to extract the core of factual information from a message which contains some structural complexities outside their normal range.

When SS have done the exercise, present the form and meaning of the second conditional using the examples in pictures 3 and 4 of the introductory dialogue. The sentence in picture 6 is an example of the conditional without the *if* clause.

Note that the sentence in picture 3 is only a question because of the intonation (the normal question form would be *If I bought more shares than you, could I have your job?*)

Exercise 10.2 Percentages and fractions (LD A & B)

Answers: *See LDT*

Aim: Practice in saying percentages and fractions in preparation for the following exercise.

SS should be able to cope with the mathematics required to do this exercise if they are going to work in business. The way to make a percentage from a fraction is to multiply by 100 ($1/5 \times 100 = 20\%$). The way to make a fraction from a percentage is to divide by 100 ($20 \div 100 = 1/5$). The exercise can be done orally as suggested in the SB or it can be written.

Exercise 10.3 Setting up a limited company (LD)

Sample answers: *See LDT. At the end of the first year Dorothy received a dividend of £600, Janet received £150 and Wendy received £250.*

Aim: Question practice, reading comprehension and presentation of commercial information/vocabulary.

You can either present this information and vocabulary orally with the help of blackboard diagrams (in which case the exercise is further practice) or presentation can be incidental to the exercise. Do the question and answer practice in open pairs, or ask SS to write a number of questions and give them to another S to answer.
NB This is a simplified account of the capital structure of a limited company. In fact, not all the company's profit is usually distributed to the shareholders as a dividend. Some of it is usually kept for use in the business the next year. The money that is kept in the business is called *retained profit*. (Pass this information on to your SS or not as you wish at this stage.)

Exercise 10.4 Investing in a limited company

Answers: *1 capital 2 partner 3 market 4 invest 5 proprietor 6 trade 7 face 8 asset 9 shareholder 10 liability 11 bankrupt 12 private 13 creditor 14 public 15 firm 16 liquidation 17 debt 18 stock*

Aim: Reading comprehension; presentation of commercial information/vocabulary.

SS should be able to do this and the following exercise without help from the T, but avoid potential discouragement by asking SS to work in pairs. Some of the vocabulary in this exercise is known from Unit 8 and the rest can be explained or can be deduced from context.
NB A *sole proprietor* used to be known as a *sole trader*. The name has changed because *proprietor* means *owner* and can refer to the sale of goods or services, whereas *trader* implies that the firm only deals in goods.

The words *firm* and *business* can be used about any business enterprise. The word *company* should only be used about a business which has been incorporated, ie which is a private or public limited company. In everyday use in Britain the use of these words is often confused.

The information about British public and private limited companies is taken from the Companies Act of 1980 when the structure of these companies changed slightly. The Act did not come into effect until 1982, so books which were printed before 1982 may not show the latest information.

Exercise 10.5 Types of business

Answers: *a One* *b Proprietor* *c bankrupt* *d Partnership* *e 2–20* *f Private limited company* *g Shareholders* *h limited* *i into liquidation* *j Public limited company* *k freely, usually at the Stock Exchange**

Aim: Reading comprehension; consolidation of commercial information and vocabulary.

If necessary, remind SS not to write in their textbooks as they complete the diagram. The 'additional information' is used in the following exercise.
*NB Not all public limited companies are quoted on the Stock Exchange. The Stock Exchange has strict rules about how long a company must have been trading profitably before the company's shares can be sold there. When a company's share are sold at the Stock Exchange for the first time, this is known as 'going public'. Not all companies choose to go public and in Britain a company can still be a public limited company without going public!

The abbreviations in the Transworld brochure in Exercise 6.5 (*GmbH*, *SARL* etc) are local equivalents of *plc* or *Ltd*. However, company law varies from country to country so they cannot be considered to be exactly the same.

Exercise 10.6 Must/can

Answers: *1 must* *2 must* *3 can* *4 can* *5 must* *6 must* *7 can* *8 must* *9 can* *10 must*

Aim: Consolidation of commercial information relating to companies; differentiating between the modals *must* and *can*.

Check that SS know the difference in use between *must* and *can* (see language notes to this unit). The exercise can then be done in class or for homework.

Note that the pronunciation of *must* is the unstressed /məst/ unless for some reason the aspect of obligation is stressed. It then becomes /mʌst/. (In this exercise it is unstressed.)

Exercise 10.7 Unlikely possibilities (LD A & B)

Answers: *See LDT*

Aim: Presentation/further practice of the second conditional; further practice of *going to*.

Present the second conditional from the introductory dialogue if you have not already done so (see note to Exercise 10.1). Then do this drill in open and then closed pairs. Note that only two SS say the three lines.
WB Exercise 10b gives further practice of conditional sentences.

Exercise 10.8 Problem-solving

Answers: The SS can choose any answers they like as long as they are legally possible and they can justify them. The arguments in each case are:

1 You could start a new shop. It could either be a sole proprietorship owned by you or your spouse, a partnership between you and your spouse or a private or public company (with you and your spouse as principal shareholders and directors). If you formed a limited company, you might find other people to invest money. The tax advantages would be greater if you formed a sole proprietorship or a partnership and possibly considered changing to a limited company after about two years. Even if you were a limited company from the beginning, the bank would probably insist that you guaranteed the loan personally (even if the company went into liquidation, you would still be liable to pay back the money), but your liability to your suppliers would be limited.

You could consider buying out the old lady's shop so that she could retire – or going into partnership with her or setting up a limited company with her as a shareholder. Note that if she died, a partnership would have to be dissolved, but a limited company could continue to trade as long as you still had at least two shareholders (you and your spouse). One question to consider in relation to the old lady is how much the local people like shopping with her or how much they are in need of a new shop.

2 You cannot start a sole proprietorship, but you could start a partnership (with 2, 3 or 4 partners) or a private or public limited liability company. The fact that one couple has two children is irrelevant to the type of business you start, but it might affect the working hours of one couple. The amount of money you take out of the business is not related to the type of business you start.

3 You could start a sole proprietorship, or possibly a partnership with your father. It is unlikely for this sort of business that you would want to be a limited company. If you were a partnership, your father would share in the risk and in the profit. If you were a sole proprietor you would presumably pay your father a straight interest repayment (hopefully at better rates than you would get from the bank).

Aim: Consolidation of commercial information; free practice of second conditional.

Note that these are hypothetical situations which are not an immediate possibility for any of the class and so it is natural to talk in the second conditional (particularly as there are a number of questions that are not made clear, so the SS have to decide what they would do according to a number of different possibilities).

One way of doing this exercise is to divide the SS into groups of four or five and give each of them one of the problems. Each group decides what it would do and then each group in turn must present their decision to the rest of the class, with justifications, and be prepared to answer questions from other class members who query that decision (each group should, therefore, have thought about the other problems so that they can ask questions).

The only type of correction that should be allowed to interrupt the discussion is the correction of second conditional mistakes.

Exercise 10.9 A Memorandum of Association

Sample answer (using the official terminology):

1 The name of the company is Rainwear Ltd.

2 The registered office of the company will be situated in England.

3 The objects for which the company is established are 'to manufacture and sell umbrellas'.

4 The liability of the members is limited.

5 The share capital of the company is ten thousand pounds divided into ten thousand shares of one pound each.

We, the several persons whose names and address are subscribed are desirous of being formed into a company, in pursuance of this Memorandum of Association, and we respectively agree to take the number of shares in the capital of the company set opposite our respective names.

1 Ron White of Portsmouth in the county of Hampshire - Merchant	5,000
2 Michael Lee of Southsea in the county of Hampshire - Merchant	3,000
3 Mara Heard of Gosport in the county of Hampshire - Merchant	2,000
Total shares taken	10,000

Dated the 8th day of June 1980

Aim: Presentation of commercial information.

Although the above example of a Memorandum of Association includes the official terminology, accept from your SS a Memorandum giving this information in simpler terms. The discussion about the company the SS want to set up should be in English as much as possible and SS should be reminded that the company must be in England (the rules for setting up the equivalent of limited companies vary from country to country).

There is no standard format for the Articles of Association because they detail the day-to-day running of the company, how often official meetings are to be held, who is responsible for what jobs, how many people must be at a meeting etc – and these details are very different from company to company.

Exercise 10.10 Describing a graph (LD)

Answers: *See LDT*

Aim: Describing graphs in the simple past.
The example sentences give SS enough information to be able to do this exercise. Do the exercise in open pairs.
WB Exercise 10c gives further practice in graphs.

Exercise 10.11 Graphs

Aim: Fluency practice; further practice of describing graphs.

Do this exercise exactly as it is described in the SB. See also the note on whole class activities on TB pages xx–xxi.

Exercise 10.12 A simulation: Speculating

The tapescript for the fifth, sixth and seventh trading periods (which does not appear in the SB) is as follows:
And now the share prices for the fifth trading period.
ABC plc continued to go down and closed at 100.
DEF plc remained stable at 200.
GHI plc also remained stable at 250.
KLM plc rose by 100 points to 500.
NOP plc showed a spectacular rise of 600 points and closed at 800.
And the new company QRS plc fell by 50 per cent to 50.
And that is the end of the share prices for the fifth trading period.

The share prices for trading period six.
ABC doubled and closed at 200.
DEF remained stable for the second period at 200.
GHI rose by 150 to 400.
KLM dropped to 400.
NOP continued to rise and closed at 1000.
QRS recovered and closed at 100.
That is the end of the share prices for trading period six.

The share prices for trading period seven.
ABC rose to 250.
DEF also rose to 250.
GHI fell to 250.
KLM rose by 100 to 500.
NOP went into liquidation late yesterday afternoon.
QRS rose to 125.
That is the end of the seventh and final trading period.

Aim: Consolidation of commercial information, listening comprehension, fluency practice.

See notes on simulations on TB page xxi. The exercise should be self-explanatory from the SB, but SS may need reminding not

... in their textbooks. However, the value of £1,000 ...ted in each of the companies at each stage is the following:

	...th trading period	Sixth trading period	Seventh trading peri...
ABC:	£800 (– £200)	£2,000 (+ £1,000)	£1,250 (+ £250)
DEF:	£1,000 (–)	£1,000 (–)	£1,250 (+ £250)
GHI:	£1,000 (–)	£1,600 (+ £600)	£625
KLM:	£1,250 (+ £250)	£800 (– £200)	£1,250 (+ £250)
NOP:	£4,000 (+ £3,000)	£1,250 (+ £250)	Lose £1,000 invested
QRS:	£500 (– £500)	£2,000 (+ £1,000)	£1,250 (+ £250)

Note particularly that the SS each have £3,000 overall to invest, £1,000 at each trading period. They cannot invest money they have won or lost in previous trading periods (the mathematics would become too complicated!).

LABORATORY DRILLS TAPESCRIPT

Drill 10.2A

Say these fractions as percentages, like this:

P: A third
R: *Thirty-three and a third per cent*

Now you try.

P: A half
R: *Fifty per cent*
P: A quarter
R: *Twenty-five per cent*
P: Two thirds
R: *Sixty-six and two-thirds per cent*
P: Three quarters
R: *Seventy-five per cent*
P: One
R: *A hundred per cent*

P: A fifth
R: *Twenty per cent*
P: A tenth
R: *Ten per cent*
P: Nine tenths
R: *Ninety per cent*
P: Four fifths
R: *Eighty per cent*
P: A hundredth
R: *One per cent*

Aim: Recognition of fractions and practice of percentages
NB Fractions of percentages can also be said as decimals, eg *thirty-three point three per cent* (or more exactly, *thirty-three point three* recurring)

Drill 10.2B

Say these percentages as fractions, like this:

P: Thirty-three and a third per cent
R: *A third*

Now you try.

P: Twenty-five per cent
R: *A quarter*
P: Fifty per cent
R: *A half*
P: Sixty-six and two-thirds per cent
R: *Two thirds*
P: A hundred per cent
R: *One*
P: Ten per cent
R: *A tenth*

P: Twenty per cent
R: *A fifth*
P: Ninety per cent
R: *Nine tenths*
P: Seventy-five per cent
R: *Three quarters*
P: One per cent
R: *A hundredth*
P: Eighty per cent
R: *Four fifths*

Aim: Recognition of percentages and practice of fractions
NB The order of the percentages has been changed so SS cannot do the drill mechanically from the book.

Drill 10.3

Give short answers to these questions about WJD Limited in Exercise 10.3, like this:

P: Who is the majority shareholder?
R: *Dorothy*

Now you try.
(The example is not repeated on the tape)

P: What is the par value of Janet's shares?
R: *One thousand, five hundred pounds*
P: How much did Wendy invest?
R: *Two thousand, five hundred pounds*
P: Who has the controlling interest in WJD Ltd?
R: *Dorothy*
P: How much is the capital of WJD Ltd?
R: *Ten thousand pounds*
P: How many shares has WJD Ltd issued?
R: *Twenty thousand*
P: What is the par value of each share?
R: *Fifty pence*
P: What is the face value of Wendy's shares?
R: *Two thousand, five hundred pounds*
P: How many shares does Wendy own?
R: *Five thousand*
P: How much profit did WJD Ltd announce after a year?
R: *One thousand pounds*

Aim: Comprehension of new vocabulary and practice of numbers

Drill 10.7A

Respond to these statements, like this:

P: If you buy shares, you'll own part of the company.
R: *I'm not going to buy shares.*

Now you try.

P: If you start a business, you'll need capital.
R: *I'm not going to start a business.*
P: If the bank gives you a loan, you'll pay interest on it.
R: *The bank isn't going to give me a loan.*
P: You'll have unlimited liability if you start a partnership.
R: *I'm not going to start a partnership.*
P: If you buy shares, you'll be a shareholder.
R: *I'm not going to buy shares.*
P: You'll be a partner if you invest in a partnership.
R: *I'm not going to invest in a partnership.*
P: If the limited company fails, you'll only lose the value of your shares.
R: *The limited company isn't going to fail.*
P: If you buy a controlling interest, it'll cost you several thousand pounds.
R: *I'm not going to buy a controlling interest.*

Aim: Practice of *going to* to express intention

Drill 10.7B

Re-phrase these possibilities to show that they are unlikely, like this:

P: If you buy shares, you'll own part of the company.
R: *If you bought shares, you'd own part of the company.*

Now you try.

P: If you start a business, you'll need capital.
R: *If you started a business, you'd need capital.*
P: If the bank gives you a loan, you'll pay interest on it.
R: *If the bank gave you a loan, you'd pay interest on it.*
P: You'll have unlimited liability if you start a partnership.
R: *You'd have unlimited liability if you started a partnership.*
P: If you buy shares, you'll be a shareholder.
R: *If you bought shares, you'd be a shareholder.*
P: You'll be a partner if you invest in a partnership.
R: *You'd be a partner if you invested in a partnership.*
P: If the limited company fails, you'll only lose the value of your shares.
R: *If the limited company failed, you'd only lose the value of your shares.*
P: If you buy a controlling interest, it'll cost you several thousand pounds.
R: *If you bought a controlling interest, it'd cost you several thousand pounds.*

Aim: Practice of the form of the second conditional

Drill 10.10

Give full replies to these questions using *went up* or *went down*, like this:

P: Did share prices fall in January?
R: *Yes. They went down sharply.*

Now you try.

P: Did share prices rise in February?
R: *Yes. They went up slightly.*
P: Did share prices rise in April?
R: *Yes. They went up sharply.*
P: Did share prices fall in June?
R: *Yes. They went down slightly.*
P: Did share prices fall in July?
R: *Yes. They went down sharply.*
P: Did share prices fall in September?
R: *Yes. They went down slightly.*
P: Did share prices rise in October?
R: *Yes. They went up slightly.*
P: Did share prices rise in November?
R: *Yes. They went up slightly.*
P: Did share prices rise in December?
R: *Yes. They went up sharply.*

Aim: Practice in describing a graph

WORKBOOK ANSWERS

Exercise 10a Odd-man-out

1 *has* (the others are from the verb *be*) 2 *our* (the only possessive) 3 *furniture* (mass noun) 4 *must* (the only

modal) 5 *how* (the only question word) 6 *price* (the only noun) 7 *she* (the only subject pronoun) 8 *limited* (not a type of business) 9 *was* (it cannot be contracted)

Exercise 10b Conditional sentences

Samples sentences: *2 You will make more money if you buy more shares. 3 You would not buy many more shares if you lost money. 4 You might make money if you buy shares. 5 If you sold more shares, you might make money. 6 You would not make money if you lost shares.*

Exercise 10c Graph

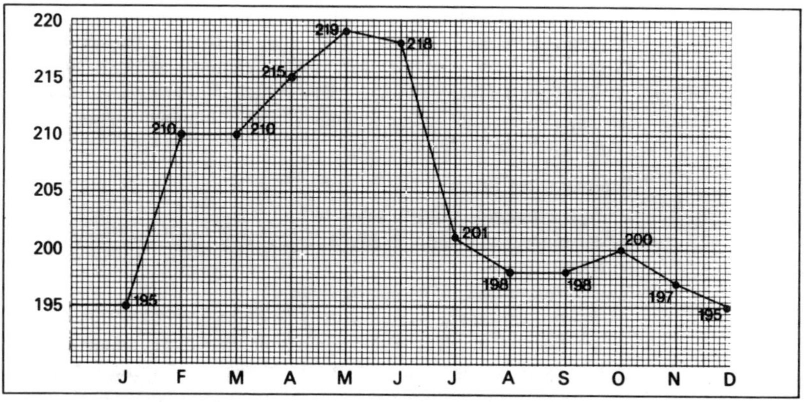

CONSOLIDATION B

TRANSWORLD NEWS

B

See note on consolidation pages on TB page xii.

Exercise B Business News

Answers: *1 Item 3; Transworld should expect to handle more imports than exports because goods will be more expensive for foreigners who have to pay in pounds. 2 Item 4 3 Item 2 about interest rates going up. 4 2–6–5–1–3 5 Item 2: interest rates going up is good news for savers and bad news for borrowers.*

Do you know? article

Helsinki–Finland; Riyadh–Saudi Arabia; Lima–Peru; Athens–Greece; Vienna–Austria; Brussels–Belgium; Tokyo–Japan; Washington DC–the USA; Cairo–Egypt; Edinburgh–Scotland; Stockholm–Sweden; Moscow–the USSR; Canberra–Australia; Warsaw–Poland; Rome–Italy

Punctuation article

a) refers to more than one customer

There is too much space between 'Stars' and 'and' and 'and' and 'Stripes'.

The secretary said, 'The boss is wrong.'

At the bottom of the page it says 'The editor invites you to write an article . . .' etc. If it is appropriate in your class, suggest that the SS write a page for Transworld News, containing interesting information or puzzles in English, a summary of current news items for 'News in Brief' etc.

WORKBOOK ANSWERS

Test B *1–c 2–b 3–c 4–a 5–d 6–b 7–a 8–d 9–c 10–c 11–a 12–b 13–b 14–c 15–a*

UNIT ELEVEN

AIRFREIGHT

11

Language:	Deduction: *might be/can't be/must be* Vocabulary development (*instruct–instructions*)
Business/Commerce:	Telephone arrangements for airfreight consignments An air waybill Flight departures Telex abbreviations Writing telexes

TEACHING NOTES

Exercise 11.1 A telephone conversation

Answers: *See SB tapescript (although SS probably will not write exactly the same words).*

Aim: Reading comprehension, dialogue building, listening comprehension.

Discuss the picture dialogue on SB page 89 with the SS and ask general comprehension questions before they do the exercise – preferably working in pairs. The pictures do not cover the whole of the taped dialogue, but the last section is exploited in Exercise 11.3.

Exercise 11.2 An air waybill

Answers: *1 BOS Ltd 2 Casolo-Ginelli SpA 3 Manchester 4 Milan 5 Three 6 1.5 cu m 7 40 k (120 ÷ 3) 8 BOS/CAS. GIN/MILAN 1/3 (on the first box; 2/3 on the second and 3/3 on the third) 9 Three (see note under C.M. Brown's signature) 10 No (in top right-hand corner it says 'copy/substitute of original') 11 Sterling (British pounds) 12 £2.06½p 13 £3 to the airline (the carrier) and £1.25 to the agent who arranged the consignment. 14 Nothing, the charges are 'prepaid'.*

Aim: Comprehension of an air waybill.

Before SS do this exercise, divide them into small groups with their books closed. Ask them to imagine what information they want on their 'air ticket and receipt' (a) if they are the sender (b) if they are the receiver (c) if they are the airline. Then compare the information they suggest with what is on the waybill. If their information is not on the waybill, ask them to suggest why not. SS frequently suggest anything to do with the transaction without really considering what is important for the ticket and transportation (for example, the cost of the consignment is important for insurance purposes, but as long as it does not exceed the normal amount of compensation the airline will pay if the goods are lost or damaged, it is not necessary to write the value on the waybill.) Ask the SS what sorts of goods would have a value declared (diamonds, gold etc). Incidentally, although most freight is charged by weight or by volume, very valuable goods which are not big or heavy are sometimes charged *ad valorem* (according to their value). Remember at this stage that you are simply discussing *what* information is on an air waybill. It is not important for SS to understand everything at once and there are still two exercises after this one before you need answer specific questions (and see also WB Exercise 11b and 11c).

After a general look at the waybill, ask SS to answer the questions in this exercise. Since the object is for them to work out the answers for themselves, it is advantageous for them to work in pairs or small groups. When going through the answers, give SS a chance to justify their answers or persuade other groups of the right answer before you give the final answer. The more you let them work out the information for themselves, the less work you will have to do and the more likely they are to remember it.

Note in answer to question 12 that *2.065* represents two pounds, six and a half pence. SS might well not realise this at first and it does provide you with the opportunity to revise quickly how sums of money are written in English before you give them the correct answer:
£2,065 would be two thousand and sixty-five pounds
£20.65 would be twenty pounds, sixty-five pence
£2.06 would be two pounds six pence

Note in answer to question 14 that *prepaid* means 'paid before' and that the prefix *pre* usually means *before* (as in *prefix*!). SS might have come across the word *Collect* (when the buyer pays the charges) in the American expression 'to call someone collect' (you phone someone and the receiver of the call pays the cost). In Britain this is called a 'reverse charge call'; the British term for paying for goods when they arrive at the purchaser's house or premises is *COD* (cash on delivery).

As a final question, you might ask SS to work out how much it would have cost to send four boxes instead of three. They might simply divide the total amount by three and multiply by four, but in fact the carrier and agent charges would probably be the same, so the answer should be £247.80 ÷ 3 = £82.60 (the cost of one case) × 4 = £330.40 (the cost of four cases) + £3 + £1.25 = *£334.65*.

Exercise 11.3 Listening for differences

Answers: *Consignment to Milan/Rome.* *Flight no BA/AZ912*

or BA/AZ892. Waybill no 125-4828-76321 or 125-4828-63740. Three/five cases. Measurements 1 m × 1 m × 1.5 m or 1 m × 1 m × 0.5 m. Total weight 120 k or 150 k.

Aim: Listening comprehension; further comprehension of an air waybill; examination of language used to arrange an airfreight consignment.

SS should be able to do this exercise without preparation, but they may need to hear the tape more than once.

SS have already prepared half of the dialogue in Exercise 11.1, but ask them to listen specifically to the language used in the whole dialogue as it will be the basis of their own dialogue in Exercise 11.5.

Exercise 11.4 Synonyms

Answers: *1–h 2–d 3–f 4–a 5–g 6–i 7–e 8–c 9–b*

Aim: Vocabulary consolidation.

SS have already met many of these words and will be able to deduce the meanings of others. Ask them to check their answers in a dictionary rather than giving them the correct answers. Note that the words are synonyms only in this context.

See WB Exercise 11c for further work on the vocabulary in air waybills.

Exercise 11.5 Arranging a consignment

Aim: Dialogue building and fluency.

SS have already prepared the language for this exercise in Exercises 11.1 and 11.3. Ask them to act out the dialogue simultaneously in pairs. From time to time you can stop everybody except one pair who continues for other people to listen to. Make notes of errors you hear as you walk round the class and go through these on the board. Repeat the exercise with different pairs and/or with SS taking the opposite role from the one they had before.

Exercise 11.6 Deduction: might be/can't be/must be (LD A & B)

Answers: *See LDT*

Aim: Presentation and practice of ways of expressing deduction; practice of present tense reported speech (pronouns); practice of numbers and letters.

By now, SS should have no difficulty with numbers, letters and present tense reported speech, but if your class does, then go through the flight numbers and reported statements with them before you start the exercise.

You will probably need to present *might be/can't be/must be*. A simple way is to take three small objects of different colours. Show them to the class and elicit the colours (red, blue, green). Put the three objects out of sight and take one in your hand so that it is hidden. Ask the SS which one it is. As they start guessing, present the possibilities to them and teach: *It might be the blue/red/green one.*

Keep the object in your hand hidden, but show SS one of the other objects (eg the red one). Teach: *It can't be the red one. It might still be the blue/green one.*

Show the SS the other object (the blue one) and ask them the colour of the one in your hand. Teach: *It must be the green one.* Ask the check questions: *Do you know?* (Yes) *Have I told you or shown you?* (No) *How do you know?* (We know from other information – we can work it out.) Repeat this with a different colour in your hand to give more SS the chance to practise the three phrases.

NB *It could be* has the same meaning as *It might be*. Do not teach this now unless one of the SS already knows it and suggests it.

Now do the exercise as set out in the SB, either in open or closed pairs.

Exercise 11.7 A mix-up

Answers: *ADP, Spain, furniture, ship; XLN, Italy, cutlery, train; TJM, France, stationery, trailer; GBD, Greece, shoes, air*

Aim: Further practice of deduction and letters of the alphabet in context.

SS can do this exercise in pairs, small groups or for homework after a reminder not to write in the textbook. If it is done in class, listen for and encourage the use of the phrases learnt to express deduction. If you ask them to explain the stages of working out the problem afterwards, they will have to use these phrases.

Exercise 11.8 Telex abbreviations

Answers: *1 For the attention of* *2 reference* *3 please* *4 repeat* *5 you* *6 could* *7 your* *8 OK/all right/acceptable*

Aim: To teach more of the language of telexes.

Before SS look at the telexes, ask a few general comprehension questions about the letter on SB page 93. Ask the SS to work out which words they can leave out of the message without losing the meaning, then compare their suggestions with the first telex on page 94. (The list of words to leave out of telexes is in Exercise 11.10.) Then ask SS to deduce the meanings of the abbreviations in the form of the exercise, in open or closed pairs.

One of the most common difficulties of non-native speakers of

English is not knowing how to ask correctly for vocabulary they do not already know. Make sure your SS know the difference between *What does — mean?* and *What is — called?*

Before you look in any more detail at the telexes, ask SS to do Exercise 11.9.
NB *Despatch* can also be spelt *dispatch.*

Exercise 11.9 Discussing meaning (LD)

Answers: *See LDT*

Aim: Deduction of the meaning of vocabulary from context.

Ask SS to work out individually from the context of the telex what they think each word means. Check their answers by doing the exercise in open pairs.
NB *Advise* means *tell* in this context, but SS will more often meet it meaning *to give suggestions.*

Ask further comprehension questions about the two telexes (refer SS back to the parts of a telex in Unit 4 if necessary), eg *What is BOS' answer back code?* (BOS 660831 G) *The final letter of the answer back code stands for the country it is in. What do you think* G *and* I *stand for?* (Great Britain and Italy) *What time did Casolo-Ginelli send their telex?* (10.45) *If Casolo-Ginelli buy £350 worth of stationery from BOS, how much discount will they get?* (5%; £17.50) *If Casolo-Ginelli buy £250 worth of stationery, what will the discount be?* (Nothing) *If Casolo-Ginelli receive their invoice from BOS on 1 January, what is the last date for paying their bill?* (2nd March – or 1st March in a leap year) etc.

You might also ask SS to work in groups to see how many differences there are between a business letter and a telex: Telex in capitals, uses a lot of abbreviations, arrives more quickly, costs more, uses different grammatical rules, does not use a lot of the polite phrases found in letters, different layout, mistakes must stay in the telex (point out that XXXX shows a mistake in a word – see the second telex on page 94); telex uses slightly different vocabulary (eg SOONEST, PERCENT, AIRWAYBILL – these last two written as one word); telex shows time it was sent as well as date, but has simplified 'address'. Note also the different punctuation: no commas, a plus sign and question mark at the end of a telex that requires an answer, and a plus sign for a telex that does not.

Exercise 11.10 Writing telex messages

Sample answers: *1 RECEIVED YR TELEX ADVISING ARRIVAL CONSIGNMENT 11135. REGRET AIRWAY-BILL NO. NOT GIVEN. PLS ADVISE SOONEST+? 2 PLS SEND (DESPATCH) FIVE HUNDRED TYPE-WRITER RIBBONS REF 752 SOONEST (URGENT) ORDER NO. 009182 AND QUOTE PRICE AND DIS-*

COUNT+? 3 ADVISE ARRIVAL AGENT HAMBURG 16 JUNE. PLS CONTACT AT INTERNATIONAL HOTEL+ 4 REGRET YR CONSIGNMENT OFFICE CHAIRS ORDER NO. 76529 DELAYED FOUR DAYS. ARRIVING BILBAO 23 JUNE+ 5 YR ORDER NO. 82310 READY DESPATCH. REGRET YR PACKING INSTRUCTIONS NOT RECEIVED. PLS ADVISE SOONEST+?

Aim: Guided practice in writing telex messages.

If you have done all the previous work on telexes suggested for Exercises 11.8 and 11.9, SS should be able to do these exercises in pairs or for homework without preparation. Not all SS will produce the sample answers, but even SS who are not usually as good at English as others will certainly be able to improve on the original messages. See also WB Exercises 11a and 14b.

Exercise 11.11 A telex

Sample answer:

```
CASGIN 625037 I
TRANSWLD 588013 G  MANCHESTER  14/5/1983  1130
ATTN CASOLO-GINELLI
THREE (FIVE) CASES STATIONERY YR ORDER NO. 7392 ARRIVING
MILAN 1345 (ROME 1440) TOMORROW FLIGHT BA/AZ912 (892)
WAYBILL NO. 125 4828 76321 (63740)+
REGARDS LONG
TRANSWLD 668013 G
CASGIN 525037 I
```

Aim: Practice in writing a telex.

SS should be able to do this exercise in class or for homework without preparation. They will have to invent Casolo-Ginelli's order number. The information in brackets refers to the consignment arranged in Exercise 11.1.

Exercise 11.12 Vocabulary development

Answers: *1 instructions 2 despatch 3 confirmation 4 payment 5 arrival 6 departure 7 consignment 8 advice 9 requirements 10 receipt 11 quotation 12 transportation 13 purchases 14 flight; 1 = C 2 = F 3 = A 4 = V 5 = P 6 = Q 7 = I 8 = E 9 = O 10 = H 11 = M 12 = N 13 = U 14 = S 15 = L 16 = T 17 = D 18 = R 19 = Y 20 = G*

Aim: Encouraging SS to look for links between words.

SS will already know some of these words and will be able to fit them into the puzzle to help them find the others. In class as SS meet new words which are related to words they already know, encourage them to notice the similarities of form and/or meaning.

LABORATORY DRILLS TAPESCRIPT

Drill 11.6A

Repeat what these people say, like this:

P(M): I hope it's warm in Nairobi.
R: *He says he hopes it's warm in Nairobi.*

Now you try.

P(F): I've missed it.
R: *She says she's missed it.*
P(F): There isn't another flight to Brussels today.
R: *She says there isn't another flight to Brussels today.*
P(M): I've got to find Gate 15.
R: *He says he's got to find Gate 15.*
P(F): I've got to wait another hour.
R: *She says she's got to wait another hour.*
P(M): It leaves at twenty-five past three.
R: *He says it leaves at twenty-five past three.*
P(F): I'm going to Greece.
R: *She says she's going to Greece.*
P(M): I'll send a postcard of the Taj Mahal.
R: *He says he'll send a postcard of the Taj Mahal.*
P(M): My flight's boarding now.
R: *He says his flight's boarding now.*
P(F): My flight leaves after the one to Geneva.
R: *She says her flight leaves after the one to Geneva.*

Aim: Practice of reported speech in the present

Drill 11.6B

Look at the flight information board and deduce which flight each of these people is on, like this:

P(M): I hope it's warm in Nairobi.
R: *He must be on LP 193.*

Now you try.

P(F): Oh no. I've missed it.
R: *She must be on LP 193.*
P(F): There isn't another flight to Brussels today.
R: *She must be on AQ 942.*
P(M): I've got to find Gate 15.
R: *He must be on MX 251.*
P(F): Oh no. I've got to wait another hour.
R: *She must be on ZR 506.*
P(M): It leaves at twenty-five past three.
R: *He must be on EN 274.*
P(F): I'm going to Greece.
R: *She must be on MX 251.*
P(M): I'll send you a postcard of the Taj Mahal.
R: *He must be on GC 387.*
P(F): My flight leaves after the one to Geneva.
R: *She must be on GC 387.*

Aim: Practice of deduction expressed by *must be*

Drill 11.9 Look at Exercise 11.9 and say what you think these words mean, like this:

P: What do you think 'delighted' means?
R: *I think it means 'very pleased'.*

Now you try.

P: What do you think 'despatch' means?
R: *I think it means 'send'.*
P: What do you think 'bulk' means?
R: *I think it means 'a large quantity'.*
P: What do you think 'purchases' means?
R: *I think it means 'things you buy'.*
P: What do you think 'advise' means?
R: *I think it means 'tell'.*
P: What do you think 'sterling' means?
R: *I think it means 'pounds'.*
P: What do you think 'regret' means?
R: *I think it means 'sorry'.*

Aim: Vocabulary recognition

WORKBOOK ANSWERS

Exercise 11a Telex messages

2 REGRET CONSIGNMENT 76529 DELAYED FOUR DAYS+
3 PLS SEND 20 CASES ELECTRIC DRILLS REF 0832+?
4 PLS QUOTE YR BEST TERMS FOR INSURING ORDER 63759 TO MUNICH+?
5 AGENT ARRIVING MANCHESTER FLIGHT AZ642 SAT+
6 ORDER 0004 DESPATCHED TODAY FLIGHT KLM 741 ARRIVING 1830+ or *... ARRIVING 1830 FLIGHT KLM 741+*

Exercise 11b An air waybill

See page 99.

Exercise 11c Word puzzle

1 departure 2 carrier 3 consignee 4 rate 5 shipper 6 no 7 value 8 collect 9 prepaid 10 dimensions 11 original Hidden word: *destination*

COPY/SUBSTITUTE OF ORIGINAL AIR WAYBILL

125 – 6365 – 7636

Airport of Departure	Execution Date Day/Month/Year	TC	Chge Code	Currency Code	For Carrier use only	
					Flight/Day	Flight/Day

125 – 6365 – 7636

Airport of Departure (Address of First Carrier) and Requested Routing	Airport of Destination	Flight/Day	Flight/Day
MANCHESTER (LHR)	KENNEDY	BA032	24/8/83

Routing and Destination — Booked

1 To — By First Carrier: BA — To — By — To — By

British airways

Air Waybill (Air Consignment note)

Issued by

Not negotiable

2 Consignee's Account Number — Consignee's Name and Address

SPIRODUPE INC
BROADWAY
NEW YORK
USA

3 Shipper's Account Number — Shipper's Name and Address

GLM ENGINEERING LTD
10 OAK WAY
HALIFAX HX6 3LP

The shipper certifies that the particulars on the face hereof are correct, agrees to the CONDITIONS ON REVERSE HEREOF, accepts that the carrier's liability is limited as stated in 4(c) on the reverse hereof and accepts such value unless a higher value for carriage is declared on the face hereof subject to an additional charge.

Jane hong pp TRANSWORLD FREIGHT

Signature of Shipper or his Agent)

Carrier certifies goods described below were received for carriage subject to the CONDITIONS ON REVERSE HEREOF, the goods then being in apparent good order and condition except as noted hereon.

Executed on 24/8/1983 (Date) at MANCHESTER (Place)

C. Cridge

Signature of Issuing Carrier or its Agent

4 Issuing Carrier's Agent, Account No. — Issuing Carrier's Agent, Name and City

TRANSWORLD FREIGHT
74 DOCKSIDE
MANCHESTER M15 7BJ

Agent's IATA Code: 39 – 9 – 1113

Copies 1, 2 and 3 of this Air Waybill are originals and have the same validity.

5 Currency: UK£ — V — Declared Value for Carriage: NVD — B — Declared Value for Customs

Weight Charge and Valuation Charge (Prepaid / Collect) — All Other Charges at Origin (Prepaid / Collect)

Accounting Information: REF. 6308880 NY 844582

6

No. of Packages RCP	Actual Gross Weight	kg/lb	Rate Class / Commodity Item No.	Chargeable Weight	Rate/Charge	Total	Nature and Quantity of Goods (Incl. Dimensions or Volume)
4	400	K		400K	0.025	10.00	4 CASES ELECTRIC DRILLS 1m x 1m x 1m

PREPAID 7

Prepaid Weight Charge	Prepaid Valuation Charge	Due Carrier (Total other Prepaid Charges)	Due Agent	Total Prepaid	For Carrier's Use Only at Destination
10.00 V	C	3.50 A	1.50 P	15.00	

R Other Charges (except Weight Charge and Valuation Charge) — Collect Charges in Destination Currency

S

T — Total Charges

COLLECT 8 Collect Weight Charge — V — Collect Valuation Charge — C — Due Carrier — Total Other Collect Charges — A — Due Agent — Total Collect

9

4 CASES GLM/SPIDUP/NEW YORK 1 – 4

Handling Information

T334(12th)

125 – 6365 – 7636

Copied at .... By ....

UNIT TWELVE
IMPORT REGULATIONS

12

Language:	Defining relative clauses Obligation: *must/have to/do not have to/ mustn't* *Having things done* First/second conditionals
Business/Commerce:	Import regulations Customs documentation Documents for a consignment (*revision*) The function of the customs Oral (and written) presentation A simulation: Trade negotiations

TEACHING NOTES

Exercise 12.1 Listening comprehension

Answers: *1–c(g) 2–f 3–e 4–g 5–a 6–d 7–b*

Aim: Listening comprehension; understanding words from context.

Ask SS to look at the dialogue on SB page 97 and note any words they do not understand. Then play the tape once or twice for the SS to do Exercise 12.1. After doing this they should be able to understand the picture dialogue. Ask them to make up comprehension questions on the picture dialogue. A sample of these can be asked and answered in open pairs in class, or they can be written and given to another S to answer in class or for homework.

Exercise 12.2 Definitions

Answers: *1 A building where goods are stored until the duty is paid is called a bonded warehouse. 2 Money (which is) paid to the government on imported goods is called duty or tariffs. 3 A person who imports goods is called an importer. 4 A document (which is) used for sending goods by sea is called a Bill of Lading. 5 A building where goods are produced is called a factory. 6 A person who sells goods abroad is called an exporter. 7 A company which arranges transportation and documentation is called a freight forwarder. 8 Goods which are being sent by sea are called seafreight. 9 The place where goods are being sent (to) is called the destination. 10 The place where goods are loaded on to ships is called the docks.*

NB In sentences 2 and 4 *which is* can be omitted.

Aim: Practice of defining relative clauses and vocabulary revision.

Refer SS to the notes on defining relative clauses on SB page 104, tell them they are being tested on vocabulary from previous units and let them work out the exercise for themselves in pairs.

Exercise 12.3 Import regulations and Exercise 12.4 Reading comprehension

Answers (12.3): *1/2 import licence–consular invoice 3 customs entry form 4 duty 5/6 certificate of Origin–import licence 7 Beland/Aland 8 customs entry form 9 do not pay duty*
Answers (12.4): *1 Aland, Beland and Celand 2 Aland 3 Aland $250, Beland $175, Celand $275 4 No (They are not importing, they are selling on the domestic market.) 5 People who import motorbikes from Beland and Celand 6 A customs entry form 7 Beland's 8 Because Celand's bikes are already more expensive than Aland's and will not be as much competition for Aland's manufacturers. 9 To prove that the bikes have come from Celand and not Beland – necessary because they both cross into Aland at the Beland border and because there is duty to pay on Beland's bikes, but not on Celand's. 10 No. The benefit of having a Certificate of Origin would be to not have to pay duty, but if you are proving that your goods are from Beland, you are proving that you do have to pay duty.*

Aim: Presentation of commercial information; reading comprehension.

Ask SS to work on these two exercises together. If they are not able to complete the flow chart immediately, tell them to work through the comprehension questions (which are designed to lead them through the information) before they attempt it.

Note that the word *invoice* refers to any sort of invoice. The term *commercial invoice* simply clarifies that you are not talking about a pro-forma or a consular invoice.

Exercise 12.5 Customs documentation

Answers: *1 Certificate of Origin 2 Import licence 3 Customs entry form 4 Commercial invoice 5 Consular invoice*

Aim: Consolidation of commercial information (documentation).

There are a lot of documents connected with international trade. Different countries and companies publish forms which look different from one another and some even use different forms. The information they contain though will always be approximately the same. It is not important for SS to know the details of all the different documents, simply that they can look at a document and know what it is used for. From the information in Exercise 12.3, they should be able to work out what these documents are. From the same text they should be able to extract the relevant information about each document (see note on written and oral presentations on TB pages xxi–xxii).

Exercise 12.6 Obligation

Answers: *1 must* *2 must not* *3 do not have to* *4 must not* *5 must* *6 do not have to* *7 must* *8 must* (1, 5, 7 and 8 can be written with *have to* or *have got to*)

Aim: Practice in expressing obligation; consolidation of commercial information.

Refer SS to the notes on SB page 104 and 87 to help them do this exercise in class or for homework.

Exercise 12.7 Having things done (LD A & B)

Answers: *See LDT*

Aim: Grammar practice.

Ask SS whether they can see the difference in meaning between *must do* and *must have something done*. Ask the check questions for each *Do you do it yourself or does someone else do it?* Do the exercise in open pairs. It can be done again in closed pairs because each S makes the choice with each item of doing it him/herself or having it done. Note the pronunciation here of the unstressed /məst/.

Exercise 12.8 A consignment

Answers: *1 Certificate of Origin* *2 Customs entry form* *3 Import licence* *4 Order* *5 Consignment note* *6 Insurance certificate* *7 Commercial invoice* *8 Consular invoice*
1 = C *2 = T* *3 = L* *4 = A* *5 = F* *6 = R*
7 = E *8 = M* *9 = N* *10 = P* *11 = I* *12 = O*
13 = V *14 = S* *15 = U* *16 = G* *17 = Y* *18 = D*

Aim: Consolidation of commercial procedure/vocabulary.

SS can do this puzzle in class or for homework.

Exercise 12.9 Note-taking

Answers: *1 government* *2 ports* *3 airports* *4 calculate* *5 duty* *6/7 import licences* *8 trade* *9 import* *10 export* *11 calculate* *12 Balance* *13 Trade*

Aim: Listening comprehension; presentation of commercial information.

Before you do this exercise ask SS what they already know about the customs, what they do and why. Then ask SS to listen to the tape without looking at their books and exchange any information they now know about the customs. Refer them to the notes in their books and ask them to work out as many missing words as they can. Finally, let them listen to the tape

again to check their answers and fill in any words they had missed.
NB Ask SS why the Customs figures are used to work out the country's Balance of Trade, but not its Balance of Payments. (Because all visible imports and exports pass through the Customs, but invisible imports and exports do not.)

Exercise 12.10 The function of the Customs

Sample passage:
The Customs and Excise are representatives of a country's government and they are found at ports and airports. They have four main functions. The first is to calculate and collect duty on imported goods which are dutiable. Their second function is to issue import and export licences for restricted goods. Thirdly they prevent trade in forbidden goods, for example drugs. Finally, they collect import and export figures. These figures are used to calculate the country's Balance of Trade.

Aim: Practice in continuous writing.

SS can either write this passage from their notes or they can make a summary of the taped talk. Either way the exercise can be written up in class or for homework. Afterwards, discuss with the class errors they made or markers such as *firstly, secondly* etc which are useful in this kind of writing.

Exercise 12.11 Negotiations and Exercise 12.12 Further negotiations (LD)

Answers: *See LDT*

Aim: Revision of first and second conditionals.

SS already know the first and second conditionals, so they can do either or both of these exercises in open or closed pairs orally, or they can write them in class or for homework.

Exercise 12.13 A simulation: Trade negotiations

See the notes on simulations on TB page xxi.

Each country will probably want to protect its own manufacturers who have a potential market in their own country (a) by requiring import licences for those goods and (b) by making countries which can make those goods cheaper pay import duty. However, countries should not impose import restrictions on goods they need and which they cannot produce themselves. Countries can export goods which are also needed on the home market, particularly if they can get a good price for them. Countries want to export as much as possible (to earn money) and import as little as possible (because it costs them money), but trade is mainly a matter of compromise and in order to be able to buy the things they need and to sell the things they do not need, they may not be able to protect all their manufacturers. This information should emerge in the course of the simulation. You should not give it to the SS beforehand. It will be more meaningful if they work it out for themselves – possibly by making mistakes. The time periods are only approximate and you may find some sections take more time than others, but it is important to put some time pressure on the SS to get them to make decisions fairly quickly.

When SS are negotiating with one another, they should be using first and second conditionals.

LABORATORY DRILLS TAPESCRIPT

Drill 12.7A

Decide whether the speaker will do these jobs herself or whether someone else will do them, and respond appropriately, like this:

P: I must mend the photocopier.
R: *That'll keep you busy.*
P: I must have the photocopier mended.
R: *Who will you get to do it?*

Now you try.
(The first example is not repeated)

P: I must check the consignment.
R: *That'll keep you busy.*
P: I must have the invoices sent out.
R: *Who will you get to do it?*
P: I must have the typewriters cleaned.
R: *Who will you get to do it?*
P: I must collect the import licences.
R: *That'll keep you busy.*
P: I must sign the forms.
R: *That'll keep you busy.*
P: I must have the reports typed.
R: *Who will you get to do it?*
P: I must copy the documents.
R: *That'll keep you busy.*

Aim: Recognition of two contrasting forms and practice of the appropriate colloquial responses

Drill 12.7B

Look at the list of jobs in Exercise 12.7 and say what you'll do in response to these statements, like this:

P: The photocopier's broken.
R: *I must have it mended.*

Now you try.

P: The consignment's just arrived.
R: *I must have it checked.*
P: The invoices are ready.
R: *I must have them sent out.*
P: The typewriters are very dirty.
R: *I must have them cleaned.*
P: The import licences are ready.
R: *I must have them collected.*
P: The forms have been filled in.
R: *I must have them signed.*
P: These are the reports.
R: *I must have them typed.*
P: These are the documents.
R: *I must have them copied.*

Aim: Practice of the form *to have something done*

Drill 12.12

Express these possibilities as if you think they are very unlikely, like this:

P: If you buy our butter, we'll buy your cars.
R: *If you bought our butter, we'd buy your cars.*

Now you try.

P: If you buy our cars, we won't export tea.
R: *If you bought our cars, we wouldn't export tea.*
P: We'll import your wool if you don't export tea.
R: *We'd import your wool if you didn't export tea.*
P: If you import our wool, we won't charge duty on apples.
R: *If you imported our wool, we wouldn't charge duty on apples.*
P: We won't impose tariffs on cars if you don't charge duty on apples.
R: *We wouldn't impose tariffs on cars if you didn't charge duty on apples.*
P: If you don't impose tariffs on cars, we won't increase our tariffs.
R: *If you didn't impose tariffs on cars, we wouldn't increase our tariffs.*
P: If you don't increase your tariffs, we won't impose import restrictions.
R: *If you didn't increase your tariffs, we wouldn't impose import restrictions.*
P: If you don't impose import restrictions, we'll buy your oil.
R: *If you didn't impose import restrictions, we'd buy your oil.*
P: We'll buy your shoes if you buy our oil.
R: *We'd buy your shoes if you bought our oil.*

Aim: Practice of the form of the second conditional

WORKBOOK ANSWERS

Exercise 12a Short responses

3 Oh, must he? 4 Oh, are they? 5 Oh, don't we/Oh, don't you? 6 Oh, will you? 7 Oh, will she? 8 Oh, has she? 9 Oh, can't they? 10 Oh, did he?

Exercise 12b Word stress

re-*ceipt*/pay-*ee*; con-su-lar-*in*-voice/doc-u-ment-*a*-tion; air-*way*-bill/pro-*form*-a; *cred*-it-card/*o*-ver-draft; *im*-port-li-cence/*or*-der-num-ber; con-*sign*-ment-note/cert-*if*-i-cate; man-u-*fact*-ur-er/raw-mat-*er*-i-als; Bill-of-*Lad*-ing/bon-ded-*ware*-house

Exercise 12c A letter of authorisation

See page 106.

Note that this letter consists of one sentence only – but it is quite a long sentence.

GLM Engineering Ltd
10 OAK WAY
HALIFAX HX6 3LP

Customs and Exercise
Liverpool

26 August 1983

Dear Sirs

Please accept this letter as our official authorisation for Transworld Freight plc of 74 Dockside, Manchester M15 7BJ to act as agents on our behalf in the matter of customs clearance of our shipment on board SS Canada Queen which arrives at Liverpool on 5th September.

Yours faithfully

N. Storke

Nigel Storke (Mr)
Export Manager

Exercise 12d Questions and answers

2 Which/GLM Engineering Ltd 3 Where/Manchester 4 What/ SS Canada Queen 5 When/5th September 6 Who/GLM Engineering Ltd

Exercise 12e Word-building

Sample words: *part, trap, nest, pest, rest, east, partner, seat, set, sat, sit, site, par, per, ship, pan, ran, ten, rip, tip, sip, trip, strip, hip, pip, her, his, he, she, its, pipe, ripe, stripe, pate, share, rate, hate, strap, parsnip, priest, rent, pants, spare, pat, rat, hat, hit, pit, pin, tin, sin, spent, paste, shine, phrase, rape, pear, neat, rear, ape, shape, tear, ear, are, era, ate, eat, tea, pen, pet, saint, spin, stir, star, stare, strain, train, rain, heir, hair, air, trash, phase, thin, then, their, this, path, shire, hire, step, pea, sea, hear, heart, shirt, rap, rep, art, tar, pain,* . . . and more

UNIT THIRTEEN 13
QUOTATIONS

Language:	Intonation: unfinished sentences Deduction: *can't have been/must have been* Personal description
Business/Commerce:	Writing a letter from dictation Quotation abbreviations Pricing and giving quotations for export consignments Formality and informality in letters

TEACHING NOTES

Exercise 13.1 Listening comprehension

Answers: *1 Yes (Jack says 'meeting you again after such a long time') 2 In England 3 Several times (he says he always loves visiting the country) 4 No (he uses the second conditional – it would be very popular) 5 No 6 fob (in small letters) 7 No (Jack wants to introduce him to New York) 8 Junior*

Aim: Listening comprehension.

Start by asking SS to look at the photo dialogue. Ask them (or ask them to ask each other) some general comprehension questions. (They probably will not know the meaning of FOB at this stage, but they will find out in this unit.) Ask them to find two expressions which are American rather than British (*quotes* for *quotations* and *Yours truly* for *Yours sincerely* – but ask the SS what the equivalent British terms are).

Ask SS to look at the British/American English notes before they listen to the tape so that they are not put off by some of the American vocabulary in the dialogue. Note too that both characters speak with an American accent. (NB SS are asked to find equivalent words in British and American English in WB Exercise 13b.) It would also be a good idea to let SS read the questions before they listen to the tape so that they know what they are listening for. The answers are not all given directly on the tape so the SS will have to deduce them from what is said. Play the tape and ask the SS to put up their hands whenever they think they have found the answer to one of the questions. When any S puts up his/her hand, stop the tape and play the previous bit again and ask another S for the answer. Work through all the questions in this way. Since this dialogue is rather longer than others in this book, stress to the SS that they do not have to understand everything.

Ask the SS why Jack asks Polly if she's happy in her job

(because she obviously is not very good at it and in fact it's Jack who isn't very happy about her being there).

Polly confuses the two words *sometime* and *sometimes*. The first means *one day, at a time in the future*. *Sometimes* means *occasionally, from time to time.*

Note the American stress in the word AD-dress. In Britain, the word is usually stressed ad-DRESS.

Exercise 13.2 Dictation

Answer:

HOUSE OF HYAM Inc.
511 Free Street
New York NY17211

Tel (212)8756985
Telex 23150639 VW
Cables HYAMINC NEW YORK

Mr Christopher Faram
Millco Ltd
The Mills
River Street
Halifax HX5 7PT

(date)

Dear Chris

It was nice meeting you again at the trade fair after such a long time. I always love visiting your country. Everyone back here agrees with me that your tartan cloth would be very popular in the US, so we would like to place an order as soon as possible.

Could you give me two quotes for 800 meters of tartan cloth (ref J273), the first FOB Liverpool and the second C&F New York.

I look forward to hearing from you and maybe to introducing you to New York sometime.

Yours truly

Jack Hyam Jr.

Jack Hyam Jr
Sales Director

Aim: Linking sounds to spelling and grammar; revision of business letter format.

Although Jack and Polly repeat what is said several times, it may be necessary to play the tape twice. Note that Jack amplifies what he says at the beginning of the letter. The first time he says '*It was nice meeting you again at the trade fair*' and the second time he adds '*. . . at the trade fair after such a long time*'.

Ask SS to check their answers against the tapescript.

Exercise 13.3 Intonation (LD)

Answers: *1 Finished* *2 Not finished* *3 Not finished* *4 Finished* *5 Finished* *6 Not finished* *7 Finished* *8 Not finished* (The LD is different from the exercise to give additional practice.)

Aim: Pronunciation practice through listening.

When SS have listened to the two examples (preferably with you gesturing with your hand to emphasise the rising or falling intonation), play each example and stop the tape at each BLEEP for SS to decide whether it was a rising or falling intonation. If necessary, play each example a second time before they decide. Instead of asking the SS to answer orally, you can ask them to gesture whether they think it was a rising or falling intonation pattern as you did – or to clap their hands if they think the sentence was finished. This will give you a good idea of who is hearing the patterns and who is not. SS who appear to be copying their neighbours' movements/clapping can be asked to do some examples on their own. On a future occasion you could use the LD in class for further practice.

Exercise 13.4 Abbreviations

Answers: *Free On Rail; Free On Board; Free Alongside Ship; Cost and Freight; Cost Insurance Freight*

Aim: Introduction of quotation terms.

SS should be able to work out through common sense which words make up which term. Note that this does not necessarily mean that they understand them.

Exercise 13.5 Quotations

Answers: *See page 110.*

Note that this chart also contains the answers to Exercise 13.6 and that SS will not be able to complete any of the costs figures until they have done that exercise.

Aim: Presentation of commercial information.

Terms and quotations is a notoriously difficult area for SS to understand and remember. It is therefore very important that they work things out for themselves as much as possible – making mistakes if necessary. Before they even look at the book, ask them from their experience so far what costs there are involved in sending goods from the seller to the buyer. SS should be able to suggest the list of nine things in the *What is included in the price* column. Then turn to the book. (If SS should not write in their textbooks, they should copy out the chart before continuing with this exercise.) Read through the instructions with them so that they know what they are doing

What is included in the price?	Costs	Ex Works	FOR	FAS	FOB Liverpool	C+F New York	CIF New York	FRANCO 511 Free Street New York
1) Goods	£2,000	✓	✓	✓	✓	✓	✓	✓
2) Packing	£150	✓	✓	✓	✓	✓	✓	✓
3) Rail transport	£20	×	×	✓	✓	✓	✓	✓
4) Loading charges	£25	×	×	×	✓	✓	✓	✓
5) Seafreight	£390	×	×	×	×	✓	✓	✓
6) Insurance	£100	×	×	×	×	×	✓	✓
7) Landing charges	£40	×	×	×	×	×	×	✓
8) Customs duty	£350	×	×	×	×	×	×	✓
9) Transport to importer	£25	×	×	×	×	×	×	✓
Price charged		£2150	£2150	£2170	£2195	£2585	£2685	£3100

(note that they cannot complete the *costs* and *price charged* columns at this stage). Ask them to work out what they think logically should be included in each price, using the names of the terms and the pictures at the top as a guide.

Remember that the buyer always has to pay all the costs of packing and transportation. The different terms simply indicate how much the seller arranges and pays for initially. The seller then invoices the buyer for what he/she has spent on transport or packing by adding it to the price of the goods.

When the SS have completed their tables, go on to Exercise 13.6 which is a way of checking their answers.

Exercise 13.6 Pricing an export consignment

Answers: *See above answer to Exercise 13.5*

Aim: Listening comprehension; presentation of commercial information.

Ask SS to listen to the tape once through to correct their answers to the previous exercise. During this play through they should not fill in the amounts of money. Without checking their answers, play the tape again for them to complete the *costs* column (the *prices charged* column should remain empty until they do Exercise 13.7).

If you feel quite a lot of SS might still have made mistakes, refer them to the tapescript at the back of the SB and give them the chance to correct their answers if they wish. Finally check all the answers through with them – preferably on a table you have drawn on the board. Note that in this case the FOR price is the same as the *ex works* price (because the factory is obviously very close to the railway station – as explained on the tape). Ask the SS in what circumstances the FOR price would be different from the *ex works* price. Would it be more or less? (It would cost more if the exporter had to transport the goods by road or canal to get them to a railway station.) Ask the SS if they can think of circumstances when the FAS price would be the same as the *ex works* price. (If the factory was very close to the docks and the exporter had no transport costs for moving the goods to the docks.)

Exercise 13.7 Problem-solving

Answers: *1 See bottom line of table in Exercise 13.5 2 FOB (if Millco pays the freight it will cost Jack Hyam more when it is included in the C&F price) 3 $200; C&F 4 FOB (it does not include the seafreight or the insurance which Jack Hyam can get cheaper in the USA – but it includes the rail fare and loading costs which will be easier to arrange in Britain) 5 $1,000 C&F (because it includes the transportation to your country; the 'ex works' price only includes the cost of the goods and the packing; the FOB price does not include the seafreight)*

Aim: To consolidate and help SS understand terms and quotations.

By working through these questions with the class, you can help them understand *why* there are different terms and conditions. Note that the answers to question 1 are found by adding up the figures in the *costs* column which are included in each price. When you have gone through all the questions, ask SS to list the factors that will decide the importer to accept one quotation in preference to another (the exchange rate, the size of the company and the discounts they can get; how easy it is for them to arrange the transportation themselves etc). You might like to ask them two further questions: *The seafreight is going to cost the exporter £150. It would cost the importer $350. The exchange rate is £1 = $200. Will the importer accept the FOB or the C&F price?* (FOB) *For another consignment the seafreight will cost the exporter £200 and the importer $400. The exchange rate is £1 = $2. Which price will the importer accept – FOB or C&F?* (C&F – the price is the same, but it is less work for him/her.)

Exercise 13.8 Deduction: can't have been/must have been (LD A & B)

Answers: *1 The terms can't have been FOB/CIF/C&F/franco.*

They must have been ex works or FOR. *2 The terms must have been FOB. They can't have been (any of the others).* *3 The terms must have been C&F.* *4 The terms must have been CIF.* *5 The terms must have been FOR.* *6 The terms must have been FAS.*

Aim: Structure practice; consolidation of commercial information.

Present these structures by referring SS to the meaning of *must be* and *can't be* (or the language notes at the end of the unit). The exercise requires SS to think and use the information they have learnt about quotations to make deductions. If they are having problems with the form or the pronunciation of the structure, do the LDs first (in class if you have not got a language laboratory).
NB *Might have been* is the past of *might be*. The expressions *might have, must have* etc can be used with verbs other than *be*, eg *She must have worked late last night because I saw the light on.*

If it is possible for SS to do WB Exercise 13c in class, ask them to work in groups. Listen for the structures *can't have been* and *must have been*. Alternatively, you can ask SS to write a justification of their answers using these forms.

Exercise 13.9 Formal and informal letters

Answers and discussion points:

The most formal letter is from Fashion Imports which begins *Dear Sirs*. This is a standard, efficient letter asking for a specific quotation. The correspondents do not know one another.

The next most formal letter is from Deregnaurcourt Sarl. Mrs Dupont has obviously met Mr Faram. However, she gives no details of the quantities of cloth she would like to order, or which specific cloth she wants, so Mr Faram will not be able to answer her letter. She does not give her position in the company either. Notice that she writes *'Could you please send . . .'* rather than the more formal *'I/We would be grateful if you could send . . .'* She uses the ending *'Yours sincerely'* since she knows the name of the reader.

The letter from Household Designs is still a business letter, but the correspondents obviously know one another personally and therefore the writer refers to their two families as well as the business matter. The tone of the letter is much less formal than the others (the writer uses first names and uses contractions in the letter), but it is still laid out properly and contains all the relevant business information so that it could be dealt with by someone else if necessary.

The letter from Transworld is a personal letter written on the company's paper. The correspondents are on first name terms and, because there is no business content and no one else will need to read it, many of the features of a business letter are missing (reader's address, writer's name and title, references). The closing salutations *All the best* and *Best wishes* are perfectly acceptable between friends and acquaintances.

Aim: The important thing is for SS to realise that letters are written between real people (not textbook writers or examiners). The 'rules' for writing business letters have evolved from practical convenience (see TB page 17 and 67–8) and politeness, but the important thing is always to remember the effect of your letter on the reader. If the reader is a stranger, he/she will want only enough information to allow him/her to reply or conduct business smoothly. As people get to know their business acquaintances better, though, their language to one another will become less formal – and this in fact is more polite than remaining distant and formal! By doing this exercise, SS might be encouraged to think more about what they write in letters, rather than simply repeating stock phrases that they have learnt. The aim of the exercise is not that SS should always hereafter write informal letters, simply that they know there are degrees of formality and that before they start to write any letter they should first think how formal it ought to be.

Exercise 13.10 Personal description

Sample answer: *Jack Hyam Jr is the Sales Director of an American company called House of Hyam Inc which sells cloth. The company probably belongs to his family. He is good at his job and patient with his employees. He travels abroad quite a lot.*
He is about 45, of medium height and build, has short fair hair and wears glasses. He usually wears a suit and tie to the office. His father's name is also Jack Hyam (Senior).

Aim: Practice of personal description; further emphasis on the idea that business and commerce are carried on by real people.

Ask SS to work in small groups to pool the information they have about Jack Hyam. Work with the whole class to build up a sample paragraph on the board. Do not try to write a perfect paragraph the first time round. Write up the suggestions you get and then ask SS to suggest ways of improving the paragraph on the board by adding or reordering the information or by correcting or improving the grammar or vocabulary.

Exercise 13.11 Imagining people

There are no given answers to this exercise. It is up to SS to use their imagination and clues in the letters. It is useful for SS to build up a picture of the people they are writing to as this should help them imagine the effect their letters might have on their reader. It might help SS if you ask them to imagine friends of theirs or their parents or people they know in business, on whom they might model these characters. If you ask SS to discuss their written work in English afterwards, listen for the structure *must/can't be* as they justify/criticise things they or other people have written, eg *Jeannette Dupont can't be very old because she obviously hasn't had much experience of writing letters.* If you have this kind of open discussion in class, SS are going to make grammatical mistakes as they try to express ideas which are possibly more complicated than the language at their disposal. Try to encourage them to speak as simply as possible, but do not overcorrect them – if you correct at all, limit it to structures which you know they have already learnt.

LABORATORY DRILLS TAPESCRIPT

Drill 13.3

When you hear this sound (BLEEP), decide whether the speaker has finished his sentence or whether he's going to add something, like this:

P: The address is Ilford Road, York (BLEEP)
R: *Not finished*
P: . . . YK4 3LM. The next address is 64th Street, Washington. (BLEEP)
R: *Finished*

Now you try.
(The examples are not repeated)

P: The address is Ilford Road, York. (BLEEP)
R: *Finished*
P: The next address is 64th Street, Washington . . . (BLEEP)
R: *Not finished*
P: USA. Thank you for your letter . . . (BLEEP)
R: *Not finished*
P: of the 23rd of November. I enjoyed seeing you again. (BLEEP)
R: *Finished*
P: We would like to place an order for 24 desks . . . (BLEEP)
R: *Not finished*
P: . . . type 73/F. Could you give me a quotation (BLEEP)
R: *Not finished*
P: FOB Milan. I look forward to hearing from you. (BLEEP)
R: *Finished*
P: Please remember me to your family. (BLEEP)
R: *Finished*

Aim: Recognition of rising and falling intonation

Drill 13.8A

Copy the pronunciation of these words and contractions, like this:

P: must've
R: *must've*

Now you try.

P: must've been
R: *must've been*
P: can't
R: *can't*
P: can't've
R: *can't've*
P: can't've been
R: *can't've been*

P: should
R: *should*
P: should've
R: *should've*
P: should've been
R: *should've been*
P: would
R: *would*
P: would've
R: *would've*
P: would've been
R: *would've been*
P: I'd've
R: *I'd've*
P: He'd've
R: *He'd've*
P: I'd've been
R: *I'd've been*

Aim: Pronunciation of more complicated contractions
NB The spelling of the contractions is a guide to pronunciation only. They are not usually written like this.

Drill 13.8B

Confirm the speaker's deductions, like this:

R: *You're right. They must have been FOB.*
P: I don't think the terms were CIF.
R: *You're right. They can't have been CIF.*

Now you try.
(The examples are not repeated)

P: I don't think the terms were FOB.
R: *You're right. They can't have been FOB.*
P: I think the terms were C&F.
R: *You're right. They must have been C&F.*
P: I think the terms were franco.
R: *You're right. They must have been franco.*
P: I don't think the terms were ex works.
R: *You're right. They can't have been ex works.*
P: I think the terms were FAS.
R: *You're right. They must have been FAS.*
P: I don't think the terms were FOR.
R: *You're right. They can't have been FOR.*
P: I don't think the terms were CIF.
R: *You're right. They can't have been CIF.*

Aim: Practice of the forms *can't have been* and *must have been*

WORKBOOK ANSWERS

Exercise 13a Reported questions

3 Did you go to the Trade Fair? 4 Would/Could you take a letter please/Please take a letter. 5 What's his address? 6 Does the price include insurance? 7 Please let me know as soon as possible/Please let her know as soon as possible. 8 Have you ever exported to Austria?

Exercise 13b American and British English

2 a quotation 3 centre 4 full stop 5 railway 6 cheque/bill 7 note 8 aeroplane

Exercise 13c An export puzzle

a shoes/Athens/£3,000/Ex works b motorbikes/Lisbon/ £1,000/FOB c stationery/Hamburg/£2,000/C&F d typewriters/Rome/£4,000/CIF 1 £2,000 2 motorbikes

Exercise 13d Wordsquare

Discount, charge, bill, telex, FOR, consignment, freight, licence, customs, receipt, case, tariff, ref, cargo, CIF, qty, order, quotation, warehouse, ship, goods, duty, plc, pp, enc, ltd, cheque.

There are two other abbreviations in this wordsquare. One is *COD* which stands for *cash on delivery* and means that the buyer pays when the goods are delivered. The other is *ono* which means *or nearest offer*. This is used when a price is quoted (usually in a newspaper advertisement) and the seller will accept an offer from the person who will pay the most (not necessarily the asking price).

Exercise 13e Vowel sounds

2 import 3 work 4 receipt 5 reminder 6 transport 7 truly 8 overdraw

Ask SS to check their answers in a dictionary and go through the pronunciation of all the words orally in class.

UNIT FOURTEEN

SEAFREIGHT

14

Language:	Present progressive tense (*revision*) Past simple tense (*revision*) Word stress Intention: *do something/to do something* Defining Question practice
Business/Commerce:	Seafreight procedures A Bill of Lading A Bill of Exchange Negotiability and discounting

TEACHING NOTES

Before you start this unit, read it right the way through. Then decide whether your SS would find it easier to do Exercises 14.4, 14.5 and 14.6 before they do 14.1, 14.2 and 14.3.

Exercise 14.1 Description

Answers: *b The importer is paying money into his bank in Australia, which is sending it to the exporter's bank in the UK. c The importer in Australia is exchanging the Bill of Lading for the consignment. d The bank in Australia is giving the Bill of Lading and (the) other shipping documents to the importer. e The exporter is writing the Bill of Exchange. f The UK bank is sending the two bills and (the) other documents to the bank in Australia. g The bank in Australia is sending the accepted Bill of Exchange to the exporter in the UK. h The importer is writing 'accepted' on the Bill of Exchange and signing it. i The exporter is giving the two bills and (the) other shipping documents to his/the bank in the UK. j The exporter is exchanging the Bill of Exchange for money at the/his bank in the UK.*

Aim: Preparation for presenting commercial information; structure practice (present progressive and articles).

The important thing in this exercise is for SS to become familiar with the picture sequence. Therefore ask them to cover the exercise and try to express what is happening in the pictures without the notes if possible. Note that the present progressive is used to describe what is happening in pictures. The definite article is used to talk about the exporter, the importer, the banks etc because the pictures all refer to one particular consignment. It is also acceptable for SS to refer to each of these as 'an exporter', 'an importer' etc the first time, and use the definite article once the characters have been established. The first reference to each bank will probably be as *his bank* rather than *a bank* – if SS have made that connection.

Exercise 14.2 Listen and match

Answers: *1–a* *2–e* *3–i* *4–f* *5–b* *6–d* *7–c* *8–h* *9–d* *10–g* *11–c* *12–b* *13–j*

Aim: Listening comprehension; presentation of commercial information.

It is important to give the SS time to think about the procedures before they listen to the tape or they will find it too complicated a task. Play the tape once up to the end of the description of D/P (the end of the second paragraph). Then go back and stop it after each of the three stages for SS to check that they have understood. Do the same for the third paragraph about D/A. If SS have great difficulties with listening, allow them to read the transcript with the tape and then check their answers against the tapescript before you correct them. Note that this account is deliberately simplified (although it may not seem like it!) In real life a lot of the transportation documentation would usually be handled by a freight forwarder (like Transworld) and a large proportion of goods would be sent to be packed in containers before being exported.

Exercise 14.3 A seafreight transaction

Answers: D/P: *We loaded the micro-processors on board ship in Liverpool and received the B/L. We then wrote the B/E for £1,000. We gave the two bills and the other shipping documents to our bank in the UK, which sent them to BJT's bank in Australia. BJT paid £1,000 (in Australian dollars) into their bank in Australia, which sent it to our bank in the UK. BJT's bank then gave them the Bill of Lading and other documents and they exchanged the B/L for the micro-processors.*

D/A: *BOS loaded the stationery on board ship in London and received the B/L. They then wrote the B/E for £750. They gave the two bills and the other shipping documents to their bank in London, which sent them to our bank in Japan. We wrote 'accepted' on the B/E and signed it. Our bank gave us the B/L and other documents. Our bank sent the accepted B/E to BOS in London. We exchanged the B/L for the stationery. We paid the £750 (in Japanese yen) into our bank in Japan which sent it to BOS's bank in England. Finally BOS exchanged the B/E for the £750 at their bank.*

Aim: Consolidation of commercial information; practice of structure (past simple) and paragraph writing.

The most important part of this exercise is for SS to make the decision about which method of payment is more advantageous for the exporter (D/P – because he/she receives the money immediately) and which for the importer (D/A because he/she does not pay until later). After that it is a matter of rewriting the two transactions in the simple past making the appropriate pronoun changes and inserting the relevant names. Since SS might need to spend a bit of time on this to get it right, you might set the exercise for homework.

Exercise 14.4 A Bill of Lading

Answers: *1–b* *2–k* *3–h* *4–f* *5–m* *6–c/d* *7–g* *8–c/d* *9–i* *10–a* *11–j* *12–l* *13–e*

Aim: Consolidation of commercial information.

A B/L is very similar to an air waybill and SS should have no difficulty in deciding which information should appear where. Although the B/L is issued by an Australian shipping company, it is issued and the consignment paid for in Liverpool, so it is likely that the goods are travelling from Liverpool to Melbourne and not vice versa. One possible query is with the sections 'consignee' and 'notify party'. 'Notify party' means the people who should be told when the consignment arrives (the importer who arranges the consignment). The rest of this information is dealt with in Exercise 14.8.

The small print on the B/L has deliberately not been printed – it is not necessary for SS to read it at this stage.

See WB Exercise 14c for ways of describing B/Ls to indicate various circumstances that might arise. Note that a 'through B/L' is used instead of a combined transport document.

Exercise 14.5 Word puzzle

Answers: *1 loading* *2 destination* *3 consignee* *4 measurement* *5 weight* *6 liner* *7 notify* *8 original* *9 issue* *10 vessel* *11 shipper* *12 port* *13 freight*

Aim: Consolidation of commercial vocabulary.

Set SS to work out this puzzle without help. The clues and the limited number of words on the bill, as well as their existing knowledge, will help them understand the parts of the B/L.

For consolidation of the various words used to identify the 'buyer' and the 'seller', see WB Exercise 14a.

Your SS might be interested to know that 'lading' is an old word for 'loading' which is still used in some Scottish dialects.

Note that a *vessel* is any boat or ship (or indeed any container). Just as *airlines* run scheduled flights, so a *liner* is a ship on a regular route. Most people are familiar with *charter flights*, particularly to holiday destinations; similarly you can have *charter ships* – ships which are hired by a company (or a number of companies) to go to a specific place at a specific time. Ask your SS whether the Australia Queen is on a regular route or a charter route (regular route – it is a liner).

NB A B/L usually has three top copies. One is held by the master of the ship and once the consignment has been paid for (or the B/E accepted) two are sent to the importer (or importer's bank) by separate posts in case one is lost.

Exercise 14.6 A Bill of Exchange (LD)

Answers: *See LDT* *1 BOS Ltd* *2 BOS Ltd* *3 14 July 1983* *4 £750* *5 One* *6 12 October 1983 (90 days after 14 July)* *7 Pounds sterling* *8 Dom KK* *9 D/A 10 Dom KK*

Aim: Presentation of commercial information.

Ask SS to try to work out the answers to these questions by themselves. Note that the exporter writes the B/E, but the B/E is not valid until it has been signed by the importer.

Compare the two questions:
Which company signed the B/E?
Which company does Sheila work for?
In the first question the company is the subject of the verb, in the second it is the object, hence the two different question forms. If SS need further practice, give them the following to make questions from:
Sheila opened the door. (Who) *Who opened the door?* I gave it to John. (Who) *Who did you give it to?* Formerly 'to whom did you give it?' used to be insisted upon, but this is now regarded by many people as pedantic. You should decide which form to use with due regard to the expectations of local examiners.

Exercise 14.7 Making out a Bill of Exchange

Answer:

Exchange for £1,000 (date)
At sight pay this solo Bill of Exchange
to the order of ourselves
the sum of one thousand pounds sterling

Value goods

To BJT (Pty)
Outback Street
Melbourne

Signed BRW
For GLM Engineering Ltd
10 Oak Way
Halifax

The only part of the B/E SS may not be able to complete accurately is the word *sight* which means payment as soon as it is seen by the importer. Another name for a B/E is a *draft* and a B/E which is to be paid at sight is known as a *sight draft*.

Exercise 14.8 Negotiability

Answers: *1 It is a ticket and a receipt for the goods (like a consignment note). 2 or order 3 No. It says on it that it is not negotiable. 4 No, because the exporter receives the money immediately. 5 c (The money that the bank makes on the B/E when it is finally paid will be calculated to be about the amount of the interest it would have received if the exporter had borrowed that amount of money.)*

Aim: Presentation of commercial information.

This passage should be self-explanatory and completes the information SS need to know about B/Ls. There is further practice and information to do with B/Ls in the WB exercises for this unit.

Exercise 14.9 Word stress

Answers: *1 DIS-count 2 EX-port 3 im-PORT 4 re-CEIVE 5 re-CEIPT 6 o-ver-DRAWN 7 O-ver-draft 8 ar-RIVE 9 ar-RIV-al 10 TRANS-port 11 trans-PORT 12 trans-port-A-tion*

Aim: Concentration on pronunciation.

Before SS begin this exercise, tell them that two-syllable nouns usually have the stress on their first syllable, unless there is a verb with identical spelling, in which case the noun is often distinguished by shifting the stress to the second syllable. Words ending in *tion* have the stress on the syllable before *tion*.

Do the exercise as set out in the SB.

Exercise 14.10 Giving reasons (LD A & B)

Answers: *See LDT*

Aim: Structure presentation and practice.

The exercise contains its own presentation. Give SS time to decide what they think the answers are and then do the exercise in open pairs.

Note the following time sequence:

PAST	PRESENT	FUTURE
I wanted some money.	*I'm going to the bank.*	*I will cash a cheque.*

Why did you go to the bank? *Because I wanted some money.*
Why did you go to the bank? *To cash a cheque.*

Exercise 14.11 Definitions (LD)

Sample answers: *See LDT*

Aim: Consolidation of vocabulary; practice in defining words.

This is a very useful exercise if it is done as suggested in the SB. SS definitions can then be compared to those on the tape for listening practice in class.

LABORATORY DRILLS TAPESCRIPT

Drill 14.6

Ask the following questions, like this:

P: Ask who wrote the Bill of Exchange.
R: *Who wrote the Bill of Exchange?*

Now you try.

P: Ask which company will receive the money.
R: *Which company will receive the money?*
P: Ask which company Sheila Baker works for.
R: *Which company does Sheila Baker work for?*
P: Ask what date the Bill was written.
R: *What date was the Bill written?*
P: Ask how much the Bill is for.
R: *How much is the Bill for?*
P: Ask how many copies of the Bill there are.
R: *How many copies of the Bill are there?*
P: Ask what date the Bill will be paid.
R: *What date will the Bill be paid?*
P: Ask whether the Bill will be paid in pounds or in yen.
R: *Will the Bill be paid in pounds or in yen?*
P: Ask which company will pay the Bill.
R: *Which company will pay the Bill?*
P: Ask who M Satsuma works for.
R: *Who does M Satsuma work for?*

Aim: Question practice

Drill 14.10A

Ask why people did the following things, like this:

P: He went to the bank.
R: *Why did he go to the bank?*

Now you try.

P: He rang the freight forwarders.
R: *Why did he ring the freight forwarders?*
P: He went to the docks.
R: *Why did he go to the docks?*
P: He flew to Amsterdam.
R: *Why did he fly to Amsterdam?*
P: He picked up the phone.
R: *Why did he pick up the phone?*
P: He went to the telex room.
R: *Why did he go to the telex room?*
P: He sat down at his desk.
R: *Why did he sit down at his desk?*
P: He went to the photocopier.
R: *Why did he go to the photocopier?*

Aim: Revision of the past simple question form

Drill 14.10B

Look at the list in Exercise 14.10 and explain why Nigel Storke did these things, like this:

P: Why did he go to the bank?
R: *He went to the bank to cash a cheque.*

Now you try.

P: Why did he ring the freight forwarders?
R: *He rang the freight forwarders to arrange transportation.*
P: Why did he go to the docks?
R: *He went to the docks to deliver some freight.*
P: Why did he fly to Amsterdam?
R: *He flew to Amsterdam to meet the Dutch representative.*
P: Why did he pick up the phone?
R: *He picked up the phone to ring Transworld.*
P: Why did he go to the telex room?
R: *He went to the telex room to send a telex.*
P: Why did he sit down at his desk?
R: *He sat down at his desk to write some letters.*
P: Why did he go to the photocopier?
R: *He went to the photocopier to copy some documents.*

Aim: Practice of the infinitive to express purpose

Drill 14.11

Decide which words in Exercise 14.11 are being defined, like this:

P: I sent him the . . . you know, the consignment note for sending goods by sea. What's it called?
R: *Bill of Lading*
P: That's right. I sent him the Bill of Lading.

Now you try.
(The example is not repeated)

P: I filled in the . . . you know, the form you fill in when you apply for insurance. What's it called?
R: *Proposal form*
P: That's right. I sent him the proposal form.
They wanted to know the . . . you know, the size of the consignment. How big it is . . .
R: *Dimensions*
P: That's right. They wanted to know the dimensions.
I paid by . . . you know. What do you call that plastic card you pay with?
R: *Credit card*
P: That's right. I paid by credit card.
She telexed the details on the . . . you know. The consignment note for sending goods by air. What is it?
R: *Air waybill*
P: That's right. She telexed the details on the air waybill.
The bank sent me a . . . what's it called? The details of all the transactions through your account.
R: *Statement*
P: That's right. They sent me a statement.
I had to fill in a . . . what's that form called? You fill it in when you're importing goods.
R: *Customs entry form*
P: That's right. I had to fill in a Customs entry form.
I paid by cheque and they wanted to see my . . . you know. The card that guarantees a cheque.
R: *Banker's card*
P: That's right. They wanted to see my banker's card.

P: I've just received the . . . you know, the request for money for imported goods. What's it called?
R: *Commercial invoice*
P: That's right. I've just received the commercial invoice.
I put the goods on the train with the . . . you know.
What's the ticket and receipt for goods called?
R: *Consignment note*
P: That's right. I put the goods on the train with the consignment note.
I can't find the . . . you know.
What's that document that proves you own the goods called?
R: *Document of title*
P: That's right. I can't find the document of title.
It's one of those ships that has a scheduled* service. What's it called?
R: *Liner*
P: That's right. A liner.

Aim: Vocabulary recognition

*NB In Britain this word is usually pronounced /sʃɛdju:ld/ and in America /skɛdju:ld/.

WORKBOOK ANSWERS

Exercise 14a Odd-man-out

The odd-man-out is *shipping company*. Of the remaining words, *consignee*, *buyer*, *customer* and *importer* all refer to the buyer. The other words all refer to the seller.

Exercise 14b Telex messages

Sample messages:

2 PLS SEND PAYMENT ORDER 63752 SOONEST+?
3 SHOES ARRIVED DAMAGED MON+
4 BANK ADVISE B/L ARRIVED MON+
5 SHOES PAYMENT NOT ARRIVED+
6 PLS ORDER SHOES MON+

Exercise 14c Bills of Lading

1–b 2–d 3–a 4–c

Exercise 14d Mistakes

SpA is not a German company abbreviation. There is no street name or district number in the German address. There is no post code or country name in the English address. *August* should be spelt with a capital A. Mr Heard in the English address becomes 'Ms' Heard in the salutation. *Enc* and *ref* should swap positions. The letter should begin 'Thank you for your letter.' You cannot receive a letter on 19th August if you are writing on 15th August. *Bill of Lading* is wrongly spelt. You never send three copies of the Bill of Lading at the same time (one copy is kept by the ship's master and the other two are sent by separate posts to the buyer). In any case the supplier sends the Bills of Lading to the buyer not the other way round. *That* should not be broken at the end of the line. It is too late to confirm the terms of sale if the Bill of Lading is being sent. FOB does not include freight and insurance costs. In any case if you use the term FOB you do not need to say what it includes. Hamburg should have a capital H. *We look forward* should continue *to hearing from you* or something like that. It should be *Yours sincerely* because the name of the reader is known. 'Pp' before the writer's name is unnecessary because the writer signs the letter himself.

UNIT FIFTEEN

LETTERS OF CREDIT

15

Language:	Impossible past conditions (third conditional)
	Either/neither/both
	Question practice
	Comparisons: *and so is/does*
Business/Commerce:	Letters of Credit and Bills of Exchange
	A Bill of Lading
	Revision of documentation
	A letter of apology

TEACHING NOTES

Exercise 15.1 Listening comprehension

Answers: *1 No/yes 2 No/yes 3 Yes/no 4 Yes/no 5 Yes/yes 6 Yes/no*

Aim: Listening practice; preparation for structure practice.

Ask SS to look at the pictures and describe what they think they are about. Then listen to the tape and do the exercise. Go back to the pictures and ask SS to tell the story.

Exercise 15.2 Impossible past conditions (LD)

Answers: *2 Was he on time for work? No. That's why Mr Storke arrived before him. So if he hadn't arrived late, Mr Storke wouldn't have arrived before him. 3 Did Mr Storke talk all morning? Yes. That's why Kevin didn't go to the bank before lunch. So if Mr Storke hadn't talked all morning, Kevin would have gone to the bank before lunch. 4 Was the service in the restaurant slow? Yes. That's why Kevin didn't leave the restaurant before three o'clock. So if the service hadn't been slow, Kevin would have left before three o'clock. 5 Was there a procession? Yes. That's why the traffic stopped. So if there hadn't been a procession, the traffic wouldn't have stopped. 6 Did Kevin sit in a traffic jam? Yes. That's why he didn't get to the bank on time. So if he hadn't sat in a traffic jam, he would have got to the bank on time.*

Aim: Presentation and practice of the third conditional; revision of past simple.

These two exercises, in conjunction with the language notes, clearly express the meaning and form of the third conditional. However, SS are still likely to find it complicated and have problems with the pronunciation. You could do the LD in class before SS do the exercise and the exercise is probably better done in open pairs. You could then (or on the following day for

revision) turn back to the picture story and ask the SS to remember the chain of events using the third conditional with the pictures as prompts. It is also worth asking them to write the third conditional sentences for homework.
Note that normal banking hours in Britain are 9.30 to 3.30 on weekdays. They are not usually open at weekends (although one major bank now opens on Saturdays).

WB Exercise 15d gives further practice of the third conditional. The form of the LD, which is known as 'back-chaining', is a good way of improving SS' pronunciation because they concentrate on sounds without interference from the meaning.

Exercise 15.3 Letters of Credit

Answers: *1 No* *2 The importer* *3 The importer's bank* *4 The importer or his/her bank* *5 The exporter's bank* *6 No – it is not negotiable* *7 B/E D/P, because payment is immediate* *8 The importer is dishonest; in some countries the banks might be dishonest; the country might have currency restrictions (the bank would not make a L/C irrevocable if there were currency problems); the order might be cancelled after it had been sent; the importer or bank might have financial difficulties etc.*

Aim: Reading comprehension; presentation of commercial information.

Trade is about people suppling goods which other people pay for. Since there are always dishonest people, there must be ways of ensuring that the customer gets the required goods in good condition and that the supplier gets the agreed amount of money. This becomes more difficult as the distance increases between the supplier and the customer. The customer does not want to pay until the goods arrive and the supplier does not want to send the goods until he/she has the money. Also governments often impose currency restrictions and regulations to control or record money entering or leaving the country. Certain systems have therefore been set up through international banks which respect each other's honesty.

The two most common 'systems' for paying money abroad are the B/E and L/C which are the equivalent of cheques for domestic trade. It is then the responsibility of the local bank to be sure of the honesty of the local trader before they issue a B/E or L/C. If SS understand this (and it is worth discussing it with them before they do this exercise), they will find it easier to understand the details of the different systems.

Note that irrevocable (as in an irrevocable decision) is pronounced /ɪ'revəkəbl/ in general, everyday conversation, but in this banking context is usually pronounced /ɪrɪ'vəʊkəbl/.

Exercise 15.4 Either/neither/both

Answers: *1 both ... and* *2 neither ... nor* *3 either ...*

or/both . . . and (the exporter can discount it at a bank, a bank can discount it at a discount house) *4 both . . . and* *5 neither . . . nor* *6 Both . . . and* *7 Neither . . . nor* *8 both . . . and/ either . . . or*

Aim: Structure practice; consolidation of commercial information.

Either . . . or means maybe one, maybe the other; *neither . . . nor* means not the one and not the other; *both . . . and* means the one and the other. Give SS a chance to work out the answers and then go through them orally, discussing any structure or information problems as they arise.

Exercise 15.5 Request to open a Letter of Credit (LD)

Answers: *See LDT*. Also 13 What is included in the price? The cost of the goods, transport to the ship, loading costs, the seafreight and the insurance (all costs to the port of arrival). 14 which port would Bruce have written to if the terms had been FOB? Liverpool. (These last two questions are not in the LD.)

Aim: Question practice; presentation of commercial documentation.

SS have now worked through a number of documents and know most of the vocabulary. When they have done the exercise as suggested, go through the answers in open pairs.

Exercise 15.6 A Bill of Lading

Answer: *See page 129.*

Aim: Consolidation of commercial information.

This exercise can be done in class or for homework.

Exercise 15.7 A Letter of Credit

Answers: *See Exercise 15.9 LDT*

Aim: Consolidation of commercial information.

Again set SS to do this exercise without much help. They can check their answers when they do Exercise 15.9. Note that the L/C can be used together with a B/E (draft).

Exercise 15.8 Vocabulary

Answers: *1 documentary credit* *2 delete* *3 request* *4 dispatch (also spelt despatch, but not in this puzzle)* *5 beneficiary* *6 number* *7 open* *8 advising* *9 valid*

Aim: Consolidation of commercial vocabulary.

This exercise can be done in class or for homework.

Exercise 15.9 Corrections (LD)

Answers: *See LDT*

Aim: Structure practice and consolidation of commercial information.

LINER BILL OF LADING B/L no. (number)

TITAINER LINE

AUSTRALIAN SHIPPING SERVICE PTY
MELBOURNE – 25 KOALA STREET
TEL: 74245 TELEX: 15925 AA

SHIPPER CLOTHCO LTD, COTTON LANE, MANCHESTER, U K	NUMBER OF ORIGINAL B/L 3 (THREE)
	VESSEL (SHIP'S NAME)
CONSIGNEE (IF 'ORDER' STATE NOTIFY PARTY) ORDER	PORT OF LOADING LIVERPOOL
	PORT OF DESTINATION MELBOURNE
NOTIFY PARTY HARBOUR IMPORTS PTY, MELBOURNE	FREIGHT PAYABLE AT LIVERPOOL

MARKS & NOS	NO & KIND OF PACKING DESCRIPTION OF GOODS	GROSS WEIGHT IN KILOS	MEASUREMENT IN M^3
CLOTHCO/ HARBIMP MEL 1/6 (for example)	6 CASES CLOTH	(weight eg 300 k)	(measurement eg 1.5 x 1.5 x 1.5)

FREIGHT PAID
IN LIVERPOOL

Smith & Jones Co Ltd

Per P. Jackson

Place and date of issue
LIVERPOOL (and date)
Signed (for the master) by
Smith & Jones Co Ltd
as agents P. Jackson

small print small print small print small print small print small print small print
print small print small print small print small print small print small print small
small print small print small print small print small print small print small print

Present the structure (possibly using the language notes), give the SS time to compare the sentences with their answers to Exercise 15.7 and then do the exercise orally in class.

Exercise 15.10 Comparisons

Answers: *1 Both are a way of paying without using cash; a cheque is used within a country, but a B/E is used outside the country; the customer writes a cheque, but the supplier (the payee) draws up a B/E etc 2 They are both means of payment in international trade issued by the importer's bank; the importer, the importer's bank and the exporter's bank must all pay a confirmed irrevocable L/C, but any of these might refuse to pay a revocable L/C etc 3 A B/L is a sort of ticket and receipt for goods and so is an air waybill; a B/L is for goods sent by sea, an air waybill is for goods sent by air; a B/L is a document of title, but an air waybill is not; a B/L is negotiable, but an air waybill is not etc 4 Both are methods of payment for imported goods; they can be used together or separately; the supplier writes the B/E, but the importer's bank issues the L/C (and the importer requests the L/C); a L/C gives details of the consignment and shipping arrangements, but a B/E does not; a B/E is negotiable but a L/C is not etc 5 An order is a request for goods, but an invoice is a request for payment; both show the same details of the goods, but the order might not show*

(See Exercise 15.11 on page 132.)

OLD AUSTRALIAN BANK Pty
INTERNATIONAL DIVISION
17 MAIN STREET
MELBOURNE

Mr Bruce Stevens
Harbour Imports Pty
Billabong Street
Melbourne

3 August 1983

Dear Mr Stevens

We apologise for the errors in the Letter of Credit number 15927. Unfortunately we have a new clerk who mixed up your request with another one.

I enclose a corrected L/C and apologise once again for our mistake and any inconvenience we have caused you.

Yours sincerely

James Fletcher

Mr James Fletcher
Manager

(See Exercise 15.11 on page 132.)

NAME OF ISSUING BANK Old Australian Bank Pty International Division 17 Main Street Melbourne	**IRREVOCABLE DOCUMENTARY CREDIT** Number 15945
Place and date of issue Melbourne, 3 August 1983	Place and date of expiry 31 October 1983 at counters of advising bank
Applicant Harbour Imports Pty Billabong Street Melbourne	Beneficiary Clothco Ltd. Cotton Lane, Manchester, UK.
Advising bank Ref no. Counts Bank plc Old Street Manchester	Amount £900 (nine hundred pounds sterling)
Shipment/dispatch from Liverpool for transportation to Melbourne	Credit available with Counts Bank, Manchester By ☐ PAYMENT ☑ ACCEPTANCE against presentation of documents detailed herein and of your draft(s) at 90 days drawn on Harbour Imports Pty

Commercial Invoice in three copies.

Full set Bills of Lading to order marked freight paid and notify Harbour Imports Pty, Melbourne

Insurance Certificate covering all Risks

Import Licence No. LHDL 66 1983 covering 6 cases cloth CIF Melbourne

Documents to be presented within 14 days after date of issue of shipping documents

We hereby issue this Documentary Credit in your favour. Small print. Small print small print small print small print. Small print small print small print. Small print small print

pp Old Australian Bank Pty
International Division
17 Main Street
Melbourne

This document consists of 1 signed page(~~s~~)

payment details; the customer sends the order to the supplier, but the supplier sends the invoice to the customer etc

Aim: Revision and consolidation of commercial information. Note that the answers are not complete. You and the SS will probably find many more points of comparison or difference. WB Exercises 15a and 15c give further consolidation work on commercial documentation and information.

Exercise 15.11 A letter of apology

Sample answer: *See pages 130 and 131.*

Aim: Free writing practice; consolidation of commercial information.

Talk about the letter and give SS suitable phrases it might contain before they do this exercise for homework or in class.

LABORATORY DRILLS TAPESCRIPT

Drill 15.2

Copy the pronunciation of these words and phrases, like this:

P: woken up late
R: *woken up late*

Now you try.

P: 't've woken up late
R: *'t've woken up late*
P: wouldn't've woken up late
R: *wouldn't've woken up late*
P: he wouldn't've woken up late
R: *he wouldn't've woken up late*
P: gone off
R: *gone off*
P: 't'd gone off
R: *'t'd gone off*
P: If it'd gone off
R: *If it'd gone off*
P: he wouldn't've woken up late
R: *he wouldn't've woken up late*
P: If it'd gone off, he wouldn't've woken up late.
R: *If it'd gone off, he wouldn't've woken up late.*
P: He wouldn't've woken up late if it'd gone off.
R: *He wouldn't've woken up late if it'd gone off.*
P: wouldn't've stopped
R: *wouldn't've stopped*
P: the traffic wouldn't've stopped
R: *the traffic wouldn't've stopped*
P: hadn't been a procession
R: *hadn't been a procession*
P: If there hadn't been a procession
R: *If there hadn't been a procession*
P: If there hadn't been a procession, the traffic wouldn't've stopped.
R: *If there hadn't been a procession, the traffic wouldn't've stopped.*
P: The traffic wouldn't've stopped if there hadn't been a procession.
R: *The traffic wouldn't've stopped if there hadn't been a procession.*

Aim: Pronunciation and fluency practice of the form of the third conditional
NB The contractions are a guide to pronunciation only. They are not usually written like this.

Drill 15.5

Give short answers to these questions about the request to open a Letter of Credit, like this:

P: What's the name of Bruce's bank?
R: *Old Australian Bank*

Now you try.
(The example is not repeated)

P: What's the name of Clothco's bank?
R: *Counts Bank plc*
P: What's the date of the request?
R: *The 29th of July, nineteen eighty-three*
P: What type of Letter of Credit does Bruce want?
R: *An irrevocable Letter of Credit*
P: Who is the beneficiary?
R: *Clothco Limited*
P: How much is the letter of credit for?
R: *Nine hundred pounds*
P: When is it valid until?
R: *The 31st of October, nineteen eighty-five*
P: How many documents are required?
R: *Four, with some copies*
P: What kind of consignment note is required?
R: *A Bill of Lading*
P: What are the goods?
R: *Six cases of cloth*
P: What is the unit price of the goods?
R: *A hundred and fifty pounds*
P: What are the terms?
R: *CIF Melbourne*
P: What is the port of departure?
R: *Liverpool*

Aim: Comprehension
NB The SS' responses do not have to be in exactly the same words as on the tape.

Drill 15.9

Correct this information about the Letter of Credit, like this:

P: The Letter of Credit was revocable.
R: *It shouldn't have been revocable.*
P: The Letter of Credit wasn't revocable.
R: *It should've been irrevocable.*

Now you try.

P: The date of expiry was September.
R: *It shouldn't have been September.*
P: The applicant was Clothco Limited.
R: *It shouldn't have been Clothco Limited.*
P: The beneficiary wasn't Clothco Limited.
R: *It should have been Clothco Limited.*
P: The amount was six hundred pounds.
R: *It shouldn't have been six hundred pounds.*
P: The shipment wasn't despatched from Liverpool.
R: *It should've been despatched from Liverpool.*
P: The shipping document was an air consignment note.
R: *It shouldn't have been an air consignment note.*
P: The Bill of Lading wasn't marked 'Freight Paid'.
R: *It should've been marked 'Freight Paid'.*
P: The import licence number was FNPJ 77.
R: *It shouldn't have been FNPJ 77.*
P: The terms were C&F.
R: *They shouldn't have been C&F.*

Aim: Practice of the forms *should/shouldn't have*

WORKBOOK ANSWERS

Exercise 15a Documents

1–e 2–h 3–d 4–j 5–f 6–k 7–c 8–g 9–b 10–l 11–m 12–a 13–n 14–i

Exercise 15b Puzzle

Mr Y arrived back first. Mr X took 4 hours to drive to Easton (200 k ÷ 50 kph) and 5 hours to drive back (200 k ÷ 40 kph), making a total of 9 hours. Mr Y took $4.\dot{4}$ *hours* (which we say as four point four recurring) *in both directions (200 k ÷ 45 kph) making a total of* $8.\dot{8}$ *hours (approximately 8 hours 48 minutes).*

Exercise 15c True or false

2 A confirmed irrevocable L/C cannot be cancelled./T 3 If you want to take out insurance you fill in a policy./F (You fill in a proposal form) 4 All partnerships issue shares./F (Limited companies issue shares) 5 The beneficiary of a L/C is the payee./T 6 An air waybill is a negotiable document./F 7 A sole proprietor does not have a partner./T 8 A consular invoice is signed by a consul./T

Exercise 15d Third conditional

Sample sentences: *2 If James had wrapped the parcel securely, the handbag would not have fallen out. 3 The suppliers would not have charged Jane for the black handbag if she had wrapped the parcel securely. 4 Jane might not have ordered a handbag from Rome if she had known about all the problems. 5 If Jane had said what colour she wanted, she would have had a more expensive handbag. 6 Jane might have bought a more expensive handbag from the local supplier if she had not paid for the lost handbag.*

CONSOLIDATION C
TRANSWORLD NEWS

C

See note on consolidation pages on TB page xii.

Exercise C Business News

Answers: *Graham Davis ... certificate for 'the ... the most credit ... which he received ... his staff from ... Manchester ... Transworld will ... standard trade and ... documents issued by ... Simplification of ... Procedures Board ... some of their ... one of the major ... we feel we ... efforts to simplify ... international ... is in Washington ... talk to the ... They are ... agreements ... winner of the ... Year' award for ... running. Fifty- ... John works ... Smiths Manufacturing ... no relation) ... Director, Mr Frank ... that he was delighted ... an efficient ... his staff. As ... Mr Smith ... pay rise ... import restrictions ... future all importers ... an import licence ... countries will have ... on imported cars.*

Do you know? article
Bill of Exchange, Free On Rail, public limited company, Bill of Lading, Letter of Credit, Cost and Freight, account, Free Alongside Ship

What are they like? article
Ms U Scheidler is about 25, tall and slim and has long straight brown hair. She usually wears a dress. She is efficient, but not as experienced as Mr Birle. She cannot drive and is unmarried. She lives in a flat in town and spends a lot of time reading or at the cinema.

Mr S Birle is about 30 and has short dark curly hair. He has got a beard and wears glasses. He dresses informally. He is efficient and experienced and he can drive. He lives with his wife and two children in a house in the country. He likes playing football and tennis and also likes going to the theatre.

Advertising competition
Encourage SS to think up advertising slogans by thinking up words or expressions to do with transport, worldwide, international, freight, packing, export etc. Do you think the following would be good advertisements? (They are all puns on well-known expressions. You might like to look them up in the Longman Dictionary of English idioms):
Transworld will give you the earth – and you won't pay it.
Why don't you sent us packing?
You'll find us in the four corners of the earth.
Around the world in 30 hours.
We'll pack it for you and it won't cost you a packet.
Better things happen at sea with Transworld.
It's a small world with Transworld.

Let us take the donkey work out of transportation.
We'll take you for a ride.
Make your way with us.
Go all the way with us.
Jump on our bandwagon.
Have no truck with other transport companies.
It's better to travel hopefully and to arrive.

Export Mania

3 Good for C and D (they still get the same amount of money per car, but will probably get more trade because their goods will be cheap for foreigners); bad for B and E whose cars will be more expensive for Yenlanders 5 Bad for A and C who will have to pay the increased duty; good for E and F whose cars will be more competitive on the domestic market 7 Bad for everyone 8 Bad for A, B, D and F; good for C and E because their rivals' cars are being delayed 9 Good for everyone 11 Good for D and F who export to Dollardy; bad for A and B for selling on the domestic market 13 Good for C and D whose domestic market will be protected; bad for B and E who export to Yenland; 15 Good for E and F (see 3); bad for A and C 17 Bad for everyone 18 Good for A and B who live in Dollardy; bad for D and F whose cars will not be as competitive against domestically produced cars 20 Bad for everyone 21 Good for everyone 22 Good for everyone 24 Bad for everyone

Do not give these answers to the SS except in cases of total deadlock. The aim of the game is to get the SS discussing whether or not different circumstances are good for them to help them understand the intricacies of foreign trade more clearly, and they will be spurred on by the will to prove that something is good for them or bad for an opponent. Players for whom news is supposedly neutral, may in fact claim that it is good (or other players claim that it is bad) because difficulties that rival companies are experiencing may mean that your own company has a better chance of selling.
NB *Die* is the singular of *dice*, although many British people use *dice* for both the singular and plural form

WORKBOOK ANSWERS

Test C

1–d 2–b 3–d 4–c 5–d 6–b 7–a 8–d 9–c 10–a 11–b 12–a 13–d 14–d 15–a